TOM MURPHY

Plays: 2

Conversations on a Homecoming
Bailegangaire
A Thief of a Christmas

with an introduction by Fintan O'Toole

Methuen Drama

METHUEN CONTEMPORARY DRAMATISTS

This collection first published in Great Britain in 1993
by Methuen Drama

Reissued in this series in 1997

3 5 7 9 10 8 6 4 2

Methuen Publishing Limited
215 Vauxhall Bridge, London SW1V 1EJ

ISBN 0–413–67560–2

A CIP catalogue record for this book is available at the British Library
Photoset by Wilmaset Ltd, Wirral in 9/11pt Sabon
Printed and bound in Great Britain by Cox & Wyman Ltd, Reading,
Berkshire

Contents

Tom Murphy:
A Chronology

Introduction

These are death-defying plays. In each of the three plays collected in this volume, death waits in the wings for the chance to show his bony hand. In each, death and remorse fuel the plot, which yet somehow drives forward to a kind of ambiguous joy. In Tom Murphy's theatrical world, we are in an almost mediaeval landscape of dark, ineluctable forces. Yet we pass through that landscape into a human and humane realm where fate is cheated and the last laugh is comic rather than vengeful. We are in the hands of a playwright whose vision is at once metaphysical and merciful, able to countenance both the great forces that control our lives and the tiny idiosyncrasies by which we escape them.

This collection suggests perfectly both the range and the consistency of Tom Murphy's work, and the paradoxical combination of the two that makes him such a major playwright. The three plays published here had their first productions within the same extraordinary year, 1985. Yet in form, they could hardly be more different. *Conversations on a Homecoming* adopts, albeit somewhat deceptively, the conventions of naturalism. *Bailegangaire* adopts the style and cadences of folk narrative. *A Thief of a Christmas* owes much of its form to one of Murphy's great obsessions, opera. The language of the plays ranges from apparently naturalistic vernacular, to the baroque filigree of Gaelic narrative to experiments in pure, wordless sound. To borrow the musical analogies which suggest themselves naturally when writing about Murphy, *Conversations* is a chamber piece, *Bailegangaire* is symphonic, and *A Thief* is grand opera.

Yet this sense of a major playwright displaying his command of a range of forms should not distract from the essential unity of the plays. The unities themselves (the so-called Aristotelian unities of time, space and action) are broadly observed in each of the plays, giving them a classical structure that reminds us of Murphy's rootedness in theatrical history. The world of the Greek tragedies, a world in which men and gods struggle with each other, remains the template for Murphy's theatre, which, for all its irony, anarchy and love of absurdity, is essentially concerned with the same clash of large forces. The tragic themes of death, remorse, and forgiveness echo through these plays, as do the classical devices of *anagnorisis* (recognition) and *peripeteia* (reversal).

What makes Murphy such a fascinating playwright, however, is that these classical, and in the broadest sense religious, impulses, are never expressed abstractly or in opposition to the nature of theatre as social and contemporary. Each of these plays, while informed by timeless forces, is also very much coloured by the state of Ireland in the mid-1980s. If the outlines are classical, the colours are all absorbed from the Irish physical and political landscape, from a time and a place that are immediately identifiable. It is the ability to make these forms and contents work in such a way that they become indistinguishable from each other that makes these plays so concrete and so theatrical.

Thus in *Conversations* the image of JJ's desperate apeing of John F. Kennedy and of the long hangover from the 1960s in which the action unfolds, are real and immediately identifiable aspects of the social reality of a country which abandoned itself to American optimism and money in the 1960s and woke up in the 1980s to find itself on the wrong, rain-sodden side of the Atlantic. But JJ is also an image of the God who has abandoned mankind, the *deus absconditus* of modern philosophy, out on the batter while his worshippers mutter in his empty temple.

Equally, the image of buried children which haunts both *Bailegangaire* and *A Thief of a Christmas* manages to be both timeless and contemporary. On the one hand, it calls up Irish folk belief, in which unbaptised or stillborn children were buried in unconsecrated ground that was associated with fairies (called *lios* in Irish, and referred to as 'the Lisheen' in both plays). On the other, it also echoes the events of the years between 1983 and 1985 in Ireland.

In 1983, the country was rent by a fierce debate about abortion, its public language dominated for most of a year by wombs and foetuses. In 1984 and 1985, the country was rivetted by an 8-month long public tribunal of inquiry into the so-called Kerry Babies case, in which a young woman whose own child out of wedlock had been buried by her in her garden had confessed to the murder of another child that could not have been hers. Such images of the 'stillborn and forlorn' find their way into the language of both plays, and in particular into the character of Dolly in *Bailegangaire* whose embattled sexuality and problematic pregnancy make her in a sense a representation as well as a realistic figure. Equally, in *Conversations*, Tom's gleeful tirades against the 'crusades of the christian fundamentalist majorities, promoting mediaeval notions of morality and reality . . . sad-eyed inquisitors, sentimental Nazis . . .' are signs of those same times in Ireland, even though the play is set a decade earlier.

Just as the timeless and the contemporary intermingle in these plays, so too do metaphysics and economics. God and the devil may be forces in the drama, but its shape also derives from a clear-eyed sense of economic realities. Liam in *Conversations*, and John Mahoney in *A Thief* are archetypal embodiments of the Irish petty capitalist, the gombeen man. And *Bailegangaire* brings that economics up to date, with its multinational factory closing down, an economic dream imploding. The layer of social realism in these plays remains constant even in the shift from the relatively naturalistic form of *Conversations* to the more fantastical elements of the other two plays.

John Millington Synge wrote that 'there are sides to all that western life, the groggy patriot/publican/general shop man . . . (that) I left untouched in my stuff. I sometimes wish I hadn't a soul and then I could give myself up to putting those lads on stage. God, wouldn't they hop!' Tom Murphy has put precisely those sides of western Irish life on stage in these plays. The remarkable thing is that he does it without neglecting the soul that Synge feared losing.

Murphy's plays have always sought to create spaces on stage that are both real and metaphorical. The White House bar in *Conversations*, for instance, operates on three distinct levels. It is a shambolic pub in an East Galway town (obviously Murphy's native Tuam). It is a bathetic version of Kennedy's Camelot/White House. And it is a poor man's Purgatory, where God in the broken-down shape of JJ will not show his face, where Michael avoids the fires of Hell with which he has tried to burn himself, and Tom lives out an eternal suspended adolescence. These layers of metaphorical space in an apparently naturalistic play are a reminder of the depth, as well as the range, of Murphy's dramatic imagination.

That depth makes possible the big things that are happening in these plays. What Murphy is about here is nothing less than a personal synthesis of the two great opposites of modern western culture, the desperate revolt against God which has so powerfully shaped twentieth century theatre on the one hand, and a compassionate, religious culture of hope and yearning on the other.

Even the most apparently conventional of these plays, *Conversations on a Homecoming*, is perfectly poised between despair and hope. The play is set in the backwash of an illusion, Ireland's infatuation with American modernity as embodied by Jack Kennedy in the 1960s, and its characters are left with little to do but scratch at each other's sores. But in Murphy's work despair is not mere pessimism, but the essential prelude to hope. A spell of false hopes must be broken before an unfrozen life can begin to flow. Michael's despairing of the absent JJ, his final break from the dangerous refuge which JJ provided, leads not to hatred but to love. As in fairy tales, the spell must be broken before love can blossom. In this sense, Murphy's plays are an extended pun on the two meanings of disenchantment. It is this sense of disenchantment, of the breaking of spells, which provides the underlying continuity between the contemporary naturalism of *Conversations* and the folkloric world of the other two plays in this volume, which deal more directly with images of giants and journeys and magic.

The absurdist mood of post-war theatre is never far from these plays.

Each of them assumes a world abandoned by God, a world in which, as Mommo puts it in *Bailegangaire*, God looks on Man as one of his little mistakes but decides that 'I'll leave them there and see what transpires'. Superficially at least *Conversations* is reminiscent of Sartre's *Huis Clos* in which a room becomes the God-forsaken Hell of other people. In *A Thief*, the classic Nietzschean gesture of man's defiant laughter in the face of death and tragedy is re-enacted in the laughing contest in which we see a broken humanity expressing its 'defiance an' rejection, inviting of what else might come or *care* to come! – Driving bellows of refusal at the sky'.

What makes the plays daring and original, however, is their insistence on moving beyond this modern absurdity. The sense of the world as literally God-forsaken prevents these plays from being strictly speaking religious, but they are shot through with a religious imagery and a religious yearning for transcendence which make them a bridge between the culture of Catholic Ireland and the modern atheist culture of contemporary civilisation.

It is not that Murphy uses religious imagery at face value. On the contrary, he uses it in order to reverse it. He turns it inside out to give it the meaning he desires. But in doing so, he mobilises its potential for expressing hope. And he does precisely the same thing to those images drawn from the modern revolt against God. His wonderfully contradictory turn-of-mind is such that he tends to take the religion out of the religious images but put it into the atheistic ones.

To take the second set of images first, Murphy plays with both Nietzsche's defiance of God and with Faust's transgression of God's stony limits on humanity. The howls of God-defying laughter in John Mahoney's pub in Bochtán (roughly, the Poor Place) may owe much to Nietzsche's imagery, but they reverse its political and theatrical meaning. Nietzsche uses that image as the ideal of tragedy and the mark of the hero who is set against the unworthy crowd. Murphy uses it to break through beyond tragedy into black comedy, and as the moment in which the crowd, the great unwashed of a mean and desperate backwater, becomes collectively heroic.

Equally, Murphy uses parallels with the Faust story (a lodestar for much of his work, followed most directly in his great play *The Gigli Concert*) but alters their meaning. JJ in *Conversations* may be a Mephistopheles who tempts Tom and Michael away from the God of the parish priest, but he is decidedly short on magic. The Stranger in the other two plays may be a Mephistopheles who goads the people of Bochtán beyond the limits of their faith and endurance (and he is specifically identified by them with the devil), but he brings a kind of salvation rather than damnation. And, looked at from the other side, Costello is a kind of Faust, drawn too far in pride and ambition by the making of a bargain whose significance he only half understands, but he also becomes a Christ, dying to save his people.

The religious imagery is equally subverted. *Bailegangaire* and *A Thief of a Christmas* are essentially nativity plays. Both are set at Christmas and shaped by the biblical Christmas story. Yet their world is much closer to pre-industrial popular culture, the Gaelic storytelling tradition which intermingled Catholic piety with pagan folklore, than it is to the modern religious sensibility which sees biblical characters as exotic and historical. The mediaeval mystery plays, the old carols, the popular stories in which Jesus, Mary and Joseph are familiar figures from your own village, Pier Paolo Pasolini's films of the Gospel, provide a better starting point than anything more awesome and distant.

These two plays represent the most serious and successful engagement of theatre with folklore in Ireland since the early days of the Abbey. Their full titles, including 'Bailegangaire and how it came by its appelation', (the place-name meaning 'The Town Without Laughter') invites consideration as part of one of the main categories of folktale: stories of how things got their names. But their folkloric world is a million miles from the fairytales of the Celtic Twilight. Their tone is that of the original folktales which are guides to survival in the hostile and harsh world of the peasant rather than of nineteenth century drawing-room fantasy. There is no nostalgia, but rather the bitter evocation of a peasant world – still recent enough in the West of Ireland to be remembered for what it was – full of widows and orphans, sudden deaths, cruel diseases that cannot be withstood, and predatory economic forces in which dispossession and starvation are constant possibilities.

The basic structure of both the contemporary action of *Bailegangaire* and of the story of the laughing contest which is intermeshed with it, and which is enacted in *A Thief of a Christmas* is taken from the story of the nativity. The Strangers on the road on a winter night forced to seek shelter in any rough place they can find are reminiscent of Mary and Joseph caught cold in Bethlehem. In *Bailegangaire*, the play builds towards both the birth of a child and the re-birth of God. Dolly's child is to be born and welcomed into the world. But God, too, the dead God, for whom Man is as much a mistake as the earwig is, comes miraculously back into play. In Mary's final words of the play, God has returned to the world. The somewhat grotesque Christ which Costello becomes in Mommo's story, saving his people with his death, emerges tentatively but unmistakably into the 'live' action of the play.

Yet these parallels with the Christmas story are interwoven with determined reversals of it. In *A Thief* and the narrative sections of *Bailegangaire*, there is a black Christmas as much as a white one. The visitation of the Strangers brings death, not birth. Dead children are a more potent image than newborn ones. The prayers of supplication offered by the faithful at Christmas become shouts of defiance and an invitation to more misfortunes. The traditional image of Christmas as a time of plenty is a mockery for the Strangers and Costello: the very abundance of stock for sale at the Tuam fair means that prices are low and their merchandise is unsaleable. The general plenty is their misery. And even the benign Christmas image of a Santa Claus who comes to children who are good is turned on its head by Costello's warning to the children in John Mahoney's that Jack Frost or the Bogey Man or 'someone is comin' anaways if ye all aren't good'.

It is hard to imagine a playwright other than Murphy who would have the nerve and the imagination to turn the Christmas story into a tragicomedy, a defiance of death as much as a celebration of birth. Yet something of that order is necessary if he is to fulfill the ambitions of *Bailegangaire* and make a kind of ritual expiation of all the nameless sufferings of all the forgotten and anonymous people of history. Mommo is a kind of Mother Ireland, and her endless, and endlessly unfinished, story is an evocation of Ireland's buried children and buried history, of a historical grief that must be named and recognised before a country can be free of it. No story less potent than that of the nativity would be sufficient to carry the weight the play needs to carry. Yet no version of that story less dark and cruel would avoid the sentimentality which is the otherwise inevitable price of using a well-worn tale.

The very scale of what Murphy attempts and achieves in *Bailegangaire* makes it a play of immense importance. The loss of faith which created the post-war theatre in the western world also became a loss of ambition. Without lapsing into piety, or even into religious belief at all, without refusing to give absurdity and terror their due, Murphy has done as much as any playwright writing in English to restore the notion that theatre should be the arena in which humanity struggles with the forces that surround life. By letting the cursed, forgotten people of history back into the theatre, he has given back to that theatre its power to bless.

Fintan O'Toole
Dublin, 1992

Conversations on a Homecoming

Conversations on a Homecoming was first performed by the Druid Theatre Company, Galway, on 16 April 1985 with the following cast:

TOM	Sean McGinley
MICHAEL	Paul Brennan
JUNIOR	Maeliosa Stafford
LIAM	Ray McBride
PEGGY	Marie Mullen
MISSUS	Pat Leavy
ANNE	Jane Brennan

Directed by Garry Hynes
Designed by Frank Conway
Lighting by Barbara Bradshaw

Time and place: The early 1970s. A pub in a town in east Galway.

A forgotten-looking place, a run-down pub. Faded printing on a window or on a panel over the door: The White House. The place is in need of decoration, the clock is stopped, stocks on the shelves are sparse, there is a picture of John F. Kennedy . . . A partition has been erected to divide the room in two, a public bar (not seen) and the lounge which is the main acting area.

The lights come up on ANNE. *She is seventeen, standing behind the counter, motionless, staring blankly out the window, her expression simple and grave. A tapping on the counter in the public bar; it is repeated before she reacts and moves off to serve a customer.*

TOM *is hunched in his overcoat, seated at a table, sipping from a half-pint glass of Guinness, reading a newspaper; his feet resting on the rung of another chair give him a posture that is almost foetal. He is in his late thirties.*

JUNIOR *is entering front door and hallway. He pauses in door to investigate momentarily the sound of a car pulling into the car park. JUNIOR is thirty-one, more casually dressed than the others (a duffel coat and a good heavy pullover), a contented, unaffected man; a big – though simple – sense of humour; an enviable capacity to enjoy himself. En route to the counter:*

JUNIOR. Well, bolix!

TOM *(mildly)*. Oh? *(And continues with his newspaper.)*

JUNIOR *(at the counter, poking his head around the end of the partition)*. Well, Anne! How yeh, Johnny! *(Exaggerated nasal brogue.)* We'll have fhrost!

Chuckling voice, off, in reaction: We will, a dhiabhail!

JUNIOR (*to* TOM). He didn't come in yet?

TOM. Was that him?

JUNIOR. No. What are you having, boy?

TOM. Pint.

JUNIOR. Two pints, Anne. (*To* TOM.) Liam Brady pulling into the car park. Well, Anne! Are you well?

ANNE (*almost silently; smiles*). Fine.

> LIAM *entering, car keys swinging, about the same age as* JUNIOR; *well-dressed and groomed: expensive, heavy pinstripe, double-breasted suit, a newspaper neatly folded sticking out of his pocket for effect. He is a farmer, an estate agent, a travel agent, he owns property . . . he affects a slight American accent; a bit stupid and insensitive – seemingly the requisites of success.*

LIAM. Hi! (TOM *merely glances up.*) Hi, Junie!

JUNIOR. How yeh!

LIAM. What's bringing ye in here?

JUNIOR. Michael Ridge is home from America.

LIAM. Hi, Anne! (*Craning over the bar to see if there is anyone in the public bar.*)

JUNIOR. We'll get all the news. What are you having?

LIAM (*indecisive*). Ahm . . .

JUNIOR. It's all the same to me.

LIAM. Had me a few shots earlier. Pint.

JUNIOR. Three pints, Anne.

> LIAM *joins* TOM, *takes out his newspaper, is not interested in it, is replacing/arranging it in his pocket again.*

TOM. Give us a look at that. What time is it?

LIAM. It's nearly eight.

TOM (*disinterestedly*). And what has *you* in here?

LIAM. Oh!

JUNIOR. Thanks, Anne. (*Takes first pint to table.*) There's only Johnny Quinn in the public bar.

Off, the town clock chiming eight.

LIAM. That town clock is fast.

JUNIOR. He was taking his mother or something out the country to see relations. I lent him the car.

TOM. I thought he said he might be here sooner.

JUNIOR. No. He said he'd hardly make it before eight. A reunion, wuw! We'll get all the news.

LIAM. He didn't bring a bus home with him then?

JUNIOR. No – Thanks, Anne – I lent him the car. (*Taking the other two pints to the table; quietly.*) He was anxious to see JJ too.

LIAM. JJ was up in Daly's earlier. On another batter. Getting mighty opstreperous, fellas, mighty maudlin.

TOM. Are they singing up in Daly's? (*To himself.*) The cowboys.

JUNIOR (*suddenly*). I'm not staying out late tonight.

TOM. What? (*Chucks LIAM's paper aside.*) And who's asking yeh?

They have been waiting for their pints to 'settle'. Off, the church clock is chiming eight.

LIAM (*a major triumph for his watch*). There, the church clock, eight!

TOM. Another discrepancy between Church and State.

LIAM. What?

TOM. Nothing. Good luck!

JUNIOR. Luck, boy!

LIAM. Good luck, fellas!

JUNIOR (*appreciative gasp after a long draught*). Aah, Jasus! (*And starts to sing absently to himself.*) 'They were only a bunch of violets, violets so blue / Fresh and fair and dainty, they sparkled like the dew / Fresh and fair and dainty, they sparkled like the dew / But I'll not forget old Ireland / Far from the old folks at home.'

During this, MISSUS *has come down the stairs (which are at the end of the hall), gone into the public bar – a greeting, off, to Johnny – and now reappears behind the counter in the lounge. She is in her early fifties, carelessly dressed (a dirty house-coat); a worried, slow-moving drudge of a woman, senses a bit numbed by life, but trying to keep the place together.*

MISSUS. Aa, the boys!

JUNIOR. Hello, Missus! (*And continues another jumbled verse of the song to himself.*)

MISSUS. Yas.

LIAM. How do, Mrs Kilkelly!

MISSUS. And Liam.

She beckons ANNE, *whispers something to her and* ANNE *goes about collecting her coat to go on an errand.*

LIAM. The partition is holding up well?

MISSUS. Yas, thanks. Yas, Liam.
(*Smiles/drools at* LIAM, *and she exits to public bar.*) Cold enough, Johnny?

JUNIOR (*to himself*). We'll have fhrost.

TOM. Shh!

TOM *has been listening to a car pulling into the car park.* ANNE *is pulling on her overcoat, going out front door when she bumps into* MICHAEL *who is entering.*

MICHAEL. Oops!

ANNE. Sorry.

MICHAEL. Sorry.

A backward glance from ANNE at him as she exits.
MICHAEL pauses for a brief moment to muster himself
before going into the lounge. He is the same age as TOM;
defensively inclined towards the supercilious, false panache to
hide his failure.

MICHAEL. Hello there!

JUNIOR. Hah, here he is! –

TOM. Oh, look in! –

LIAM. The man himself! –

MICHAEL. Gee! Gee! Lot of changes round here! –

TOM. Don't start that game now – How yeh, you're welcome,
how yeh! –

LIAM (*pushing awkwardly through them, nearly spilling*
JUNIOR's pint). Well, howdy, Mick! –

JUNIOR (*protecting his pint*). Jasus, the cowboy! (*Liam*) –

MICHAEL. Liam! And how are you?

LIAM. Good to see yeh, well good to see yeh! –

TOM. That's a fancy-lookin' suit you have on. –

MICHAEL. What's fancy about it? –

TOM. Nothing –

LIAM. You look just great! –

TOM (*shaking hands*). Well? How yeh, you're welcome, how
yeh?

MICHAEL. Not too bad.

JUNIOR. Not three bad, what're you having, boy?

TOM. Oh, a brandy, a brandy, a brandy for the emigrant, don't yeh know well? –

LIAM. Pull up a pew, fella –

MICHAEL. I'll have a pint, Junie.

JUNIOR. Fair play to yeh. (*Going to counter.*) Missus!

TOM. Well!

MICHAEL. How are you?

TOM. I'm alright.

JUNIOR (*impatient at counter*). Missus!

TOM. You're lookin' well.

MICHAEL. Can't help it. You know?

TOM. I suppose you can't.

JUNIOR (*to* MISSUS *who has entered behind counter*). A pint, please.

LIAM. A holiday, Mick?

MICHAEL. Ah . . . yeh.

LIAM *nods in that solemn provincial way, eyes fixed on* MICHAEL *in ignorant assessment.*

And how are things with you, Liam?

LIAM. Fightin' fit, fella.

MICHAEL. The farming, the rates collecting, the –

TOM. Oh and sure he's an auctioneer too now.

MICHAEL. Yeh?

LIAM. Estate agent, Mick.

TOM. Took out his diploma after intensive and in-depth study last year.

JUNIOR (*from counter*). MI5 AA!

MICHAEL. What?

TOM. Junior's sense of humour.

LIAM. MIAA, Mick.

JUNIOR. Letters after his name and the car he drives doesn't need a clutch!

MICHAEL. So business is good then?

LIAM. Property-wise, this country, A-one, Mick. This country, Mick, last refuge in Europe.

MICHAEL. Good begod, I came to the right place then!

JUNIOR. Thanks, Missus. (*He is waiting for his change.*)

TOM. You haven't much of an accent?

MICHAEL (*British accent*). Only for the stage.

TOM (*British accent*). Yes, yes, good show, jolly good, right chaps, it's up to us, we're going through. John Mills!

MICHAEL. Aw, he's making better ones now.

TOM. Is he?

JUNIOR. Thanks, Missus.

MISSUS (*retreating off, fingering her dirty house-coat*). Aa, Michael.

We see her a few moments later reappear from the public bar into the hallway and going upstairs.

MICHAEL. How's your mother, Tom?

TOM. Oh, she's fine.

MICHAEL. And the school?

TOM. Fine. The headmaster might drop dead any day now –

JUNIOR (*setting pint in front of MICHAEL*). Now, boy –

TOM. And my subsequent rise in station and salary will make all the difference.

MICHAEL. Thanks, Junie.

TOM. What brought you back?

MICHAEL (*evasive*). Oh, before I forget them – (*He gives car keys to* JUNIOR.) Thanks.

JUNIOR. Not at all, boy.

TOM. Hmm? At this time of year.

JUNIOR. Jasus, you weren't home for . . .

TOM. Must be ten years.

JUNIOR. That race week. (*He starts to laugh.*)

TOM. Aw Jay, that Galway race week!

They start to laugh.

JUNIOR. Aw Jasus, d'yeh remember your man?

TOM. Aw God, yes, your man!

JUNIOR. Aw Jasus, Jasus! (JUNIOR's *laugh usually incorporates 'Jasus'.*)

TOM. The cut of him!

JUNIOR. Aw Jasus, Jasus!

LIAM. Who?

JUNIOR. D'yeh remember?

MICHAEL. I do.

JUNIOR. But do yeh? – Jasus, Jasus!

LIAM. Who was this?

JUNIOR. Do yeh, do yeh, remember him?

MICHAEL (*laughing*). I do!

JUNIOR. Jasus, Jasus!

JUNIOR's laugh is infectious, all laughing. Ritual toast again.

MICHAEL. Good luck, Junie!

JUNIOR. Good luck phatever. (*whatever*)!

TOM. Good luck!

LIAM. Good luck, fellas!

They drink.

MICHAEL. Is JJ around?

TOM. No. But what brought you back?

MICHAEL *glances at him, unsure.*

So sudden. This time of the year.

JUNIOR. Nos-talgia!

MICHAEL. Something like that.

TOM. What?

MICHAEL (*forces a laugh*). The White House, our refuge, our wellsprings of hope and aspiration. (*Mimicking JJ/Kennedy.*) Let the word go forth from this time and place to friend and foe alike that the torch has been passed to a new generation!

LIAM. JJ doing his Kennedy bit, is it? Making speeches. (*Dismissive.*) JJ.

MICHAEL (*to LIAM*). We virtually built this place with JJ. Right, Tom?

JUNIOR. Jasus we did!

MICHAEL. Night after night, while you were wasting all those years away at university.

JUNIOR. Jasus, we did – And sank pints!

TOM (*to JUNIOR*). Sure you were only a boy.

MICHAEL. You wrote your rightest poems here.

TOM (*laughing at himself*). I did – and read them!

MICHAEL. You wrote that speech – JJ's inaugural – for our opening (JJ/*Kennedy voice again*.) Friends, all this, our cultural centre, has been a co-sponsorial job from design to décor. Mark its line, its adornment.

TOM. I never said 'mark' –

MICHAEL. Its atmosphere derives from no attribute of wild wisdom, vestige of native cunning, or selfish motive. The day of the dinosaur is gone forever, and with it the troglodytian attitude incarcerated in the cave whence it came –

TOM. Troglodytical –

MICHAEL. And as I look around me, I know that some of us will be departing –

JUNIOR. To ride the waves or drown in them!

MICHAEL. That's it Junie –

JUNIOR (*pleased with himself*). As the fella says –

MICHAEL. To seek the new ideas. And some of us will remain, custodians of this, *our* White House, to keep the metaphorical doors of thought, hope, generosity, expression, aspiration open. So that all will find – the denizen of this hamlet, the traveller in his frequent returnings – a place of fulfilment, or a refuge if need be. Something like that. You wrote that.

TOM (*chuckling*). I suppose I did. Sure we'd all have been departing, riding the waves, if we paid heed to poor auld JJ.

LIAM *laughs*.

But you didn't tell us. What brought you back?

MICHAEL. I told you. Lost horizons.

TOM. Wha! (*First wonderings: Can he be serious?*)

MICHAEL. No.

TOM. Hmm?

MICHAEL. No, you'd be surprised at how dicked-up one can get – I mean, how meaningless things can become for one – occasionally of course – away from one's – you know.

TOM. I suppose 'one' can. (*Awkward moment's pause.*) But you're looking well.

MICHAEL. Can't help it.

LIAM (*eyes all the time fastened on* MICHAEL). It could be a good stand for a fella, Mick? This place, properly handled.

MICHAEL (*joking*). You didn't consider taking up the gun and marching on the North?

JUNIOR. We thought about it.

MICHAEL *laughs*.

Serious.

MICHAEL. What?

JUNIOR. We did.

LIAM. We nearly did.

JUNIOR. Serious.

LIAM. Shoot us a few Prods.

MICHAEL *looks at* TOM.

TOM. It's very bad up there.

MICHAEL. I know. I've been reading, but.

LIAM. We nearly did, one night.

TOM. The way the Catholics are being treated.

MICHAEL (*trying to conceal his disbelief*). Yeh?

LIAM. A geezer up there in the papers one evening talking about coming down here and burning us all to the ground.

JUNIOR. We knew where to lay our hands on a few guns.

LIAM. Well, I'm telling you, when I read that!

MICHAEL. Guns!?

JUNIOR. We did. *He* (TOM) did.

MICHAEL (*laughs in disbelief*). *You* did, Tom?

TOM (*frowning*). What?

LIAM (*boasting*). I was awful drunk that night. I was awful sick – Did ye see me?

MICHAEL (*because* TOM *is still frowning*). No, I believe – I believe things are pretty bad alright, but, a baby and all now, Junie?

JUNIOR. Oh, oh!

MICHAEL. And how is Peggy, Tom?

TOM. Fine.

MICHAEL. Yeh? She's okay?

TOM. Fine. I sent her word we'd be in here.

MICHAEL. Any signs of ye doing it yet as the saying goes?

TOM. Aren't we engaged, isn't that enough?

JUNIOR. Jasus, ten years engaged!

TOM (*mock belligerence*). Well, isn't it better than nothing!

JUNIOR (*laughing*). Aw Jasus, Jasus!

LIAM. But he's bought the site, Mick.

TOM. And isn't it doubled in value now!

LIAM. Trebled, trebled, fella!

JUNIOR. Jasus, ten years engaged!

TOM. D'yeh hear Sonny?

JUNIOR. Jasus, Jasus!

TOM. Napkin-head, procreation hope!

JUNIOR. What does that mean, sir?

TOM. Dick!

They laugh.
During this last, MISSUS has came down the stairs, along
hallway and is entering lounge, now minus her dirty house-
coat, wearing her best cardigan.

MISSUS. Aa, the boys! And Liam. You're welcome, Michael.

MICHAEL. Hello, Missus!

MISSUS. Welcome, yas, now.

MICHAEL. You're looking well.

MISSUS. Oh now, pulling the divil by the tail. Isn't that the
   way, boys? But your mother is delighted, yas, the surprise of
   your visit. I was talking to her for a minute this morning in
   the post office and she was telling me. Now.

MICHAEL. We were just saying we had some great times here,
   what?

MISSUS. Yas, but Liam is the boy that's doing well. Waiting for
   the right girl. And poor Tom waiting on you there this hour.

TOM. I am indeed, Missus, the hound!

MISSUS. Aa, sure he doesn't mean that at all. Usen't we call the
   two of you of you the twins one time? Always together,
   always together. D'ye know now.

JUNIOR (*quietly*). Yas, the twins.

MISSUS. Yas, the twins. Aa, I think Junior is a bit of a rogue.

TOM. A blackguard, Missus.

MISSUS. Aa, no joking. D'ye know now. A nice wife and a
   baby and a home of his home to go into. The way everyone
   should be.

JUNIOR (*to* TOM). Now!

MISSUS. Isn't that right, Liam?

LIAM. That is c'rrect, Mrs Kilkelly.

MISSUS. A nice sensible girl, and not be roaming the world.

JUNIOR (*to* MICHAEL). Now!

MICHAEL. How is JJ?

MISSUS. Oh JJ is – very well, thank you.

MICHAEL. The time of our lives putting this place together, we were just saying. Do you remember the night – Where's the painting of the nude?

MISSUS. Yas, but you're doing well, your mother was saying, and are you alright there now, boys?

JUNIOR. Well, you might start filling another round. (*To* TOM.) *Your* round.

MISSUS. Certainly. (*Going back to the bar.*) Nice to see you all again.

JUNIOR. She's desperate slow on the aul pints.

MICHAEL *is still looking after her, shaken by the transformation that has come over her.*

MICHAEL. She was the first lady. But where is JJ?

TOM. Sure the man is dyin'.

MICHAEL. What!

TOM. Drinkin' himself to death, don't be talking.

LIAM. That's where she sent the young one, out looking for him.

MICHAEL. Did you tell him I'd be here? (JUNIOR *nods.*) And?

JUNIOR. He isn't together at all: he's on a batter.

MICHAEL. But you told him?

JUNIOR *nods.*

LIAM. He's probably gone into Galway or some place by now.

MICHAEL. But he'll show up?

TOM. You won't see him for a week. What about yourself?

LIAM (*pleasure of the anticipation on his face*). I'll have the selling of this place before long.

TOM. What about yourself?

MICHAEL. What?

LIAM. Gals.

JUNIOR. 'Gals'. Jasus, you have more of an American accent than him!

TOM. There was a rumour some time back you were married.

MICHAEL. No.

TOM. What?

MICHAEL. Free love.

TOM. Oh God!

MICHAEL. Who was the bird I bumped into at the door?

JUNIOR. Fair play to yeh!

MICHAEL. A young one.

LIAM. You never lost it, Mickeen!

MICHAEL. As a matter of fact I did. Plenty of it, too much of it over there.

TOM. What about our new bank clerk for him, Junie?

JUNIOR. Grrrrrah, Josephine!

TOM. We have a right one for yeh.

LIAM (*to himself*). Dirty aul' thing.

JUNIOR. She stays here and all: a quick nip up the stairs on your way out tonight and 'wham, bang, alikazam!'

TOM. The most ridiculous whore of all times.

JUNIOR. No bra.

LIAM. Dirty aul' thing.

MICHAEL. Why so ridiculous?

TOM. A bank clerk, a bank clerk! A girl in her position!

JUNIOR (*whispering*). And they say she wears no knickers either. Ich bin ein Berliner!

TOM (*frowning*). What were you going to say?

MICHAEL. No, but this young one at the door, that wasn't her.

LIAM. Who?

MICHAEL. A blue coat, fair, about eighteen.

JUNIOR. Anne. (*It doesn't register with* MICHAEL.)

TOM. Anne, Annette.

JUNIOR. Missus's daughter –

TOM. JJ's daughter.

MICHAEL (*brightening*). Well-well!

JUNIOR. She's turning out nice on me word?

MICHAEL. Annette. JJ's daughter. I bumped into her at the door and I got the whiff of soap, sort of schoolgirl kind of soap, and –

TOM. It took you back?

MICHAEL. It did.

TOM. Tck!

MICHAEL. No, there's a distinctive kind of aroma off –

TOM. Gee, aroma! It'd be great to be young again.

MICHAEL. You're a bogman, Ryan.

TOM. I've no sensitivity alright.

They are chuckling. JUNIOR *draining his glass as* MISSUS *arrives with one pint which she puts before* LIAM.

MISSUS. Now, Liam. The other three are coming, boys. (*Returning to bar.*)

MICHAEL. Well, news!

Short pause; all thinking.

JUNIOR. Molloy's dog got killed by a tractor last month.

TOM. Did you hear Stephen Riley died?

MICHAEL. No!

TOM *nods.*

Hoppy?

TOM. Yeh, with the limp.

MICHAEL. Well did he?

TOM. He did.

JUNIOR. D'yeh remember the Christmas he split the wife with the crucifix? (*They laugh. Solemnly.*) The Lord have mercy on him.

They burst into irreverent laughter.

TOM. And of course you know Larry, Larry O'Kelly got transferred?

MICHAEL. Yeh. I was looking around for his painting of the nude.

JUNIOR. Transferred, and *Bridget Reclining* with him.

MICHAEL. It used to hang there.

TOM. JJ defying Church and State hanging a nude.

JUNIOR. And the priest, Father Connolly – remember? – up and down here, hotfoot about the nude.

TOM. That wasn't why –

JUNIOR (*taking fresh pint that was set before* LIAM). Here, cowboy, gimme that pint and I'll be working away on it.

MICHAEL. And JJ. 'I do not speak for the Church on public matters, Father, and the Church is not going to speak for me!'

JUNIOR. Good luck!

MICHAEL. And JJ sent Father Connolly packing.

TOM. He didn't.

MICHAEL. He did.

JUNIOR (*after appreciative draught*). Aaa, Jasus!

MICHAEL. 'When long-held power leads men towards arrogance, art reminds them of their limitations!'

JUNIOR. Father Connolly called it a dirty picture.

TOM *and* MICHAEL *speaking simultaneously:*

TOM. He didn't!

MICHAEL. 'When long-held power narrows men's minds, art, poetry, music cleanses —'

TOM. He called it a *bad* picture —

MICHAEL. As far as you're concerned then, Father —

JUNIOR   'Art galleries —'
MICHAEL   'Art galleries —'

MICHAEL *and* JUNIOR *laugh.*

MICHAEL. 'As far as you are concerned then, Father, art galleries all over the world are filled with dirty pictures?'

TOM (*playing Fr. Connolly*). Please, please — Boys! — please don't talk to me about art galleries. Holy Moses, I've visited hundreds of them. You see, boys, I am a man who has travelled the world —'

MICHAEL. 'I heard you spent a few years in Nigeria, but remember you're not talking to the Blacks now!'

JUNIOR *collects the other three pints, paying* MISSUS.

MISSUS } Now, boys, yas.
JUNIOR } 'You're not talking to the Blacks now.'

TOM. Aw but do ye see? The arrogance and condescension which you impute to Fr. Connolly's remarks were only too evident in our swinging liberal JJ's statements.

MICHAEL. What does that mean?

JUNIOR. That's what I was going to say.

TOM *waives the question.*

LIAM. Good luck, fellas!

TOM. The reason, the *real* reason, behind Fr. Connolly's visits had nothing to do with the painting.

MICHAEL. He wanted JJ to take it down.

TOM. That was the *ostensible* reason. The real reason was to tell JJ to behave himself like a good boy, to *warn* him.

JUNIOR. And JJ *didn't* take it down – fair play to him.

MICHAEL. To *warn* him?

TOM. A token glance at the nude, a few token remarks about art galleries or something, and 'Haw-haw-haw, you are a son-of-a-bachelor, John-John.' The real reason. 'You see, John-John, pub, club, art-centre, whatever it is you are running here, people are growing concerned. And particularly since your trade to date seems to be in the young. Already there have been complaints, indeed visits to the presbytery from worried parents and other concerned parties.'

JUNIOR. The opposition, Paddy Joe Daly, and the other wise publicans.

TOM. 'One native son, a guileless youth it appears, is about to leave a respectable clerkship which I had a hand in getting him myself –'

MICHAEL. He never spoke for me!' –

TOM. 'And a widowed mother –'

MICHAEL. My mother never went near –

TOM. 'To go off to Dublin to become – of all things! – an actor.'

MICHAEL. Maybe your mother did –

TOM. 'While another is suddenly contemplating leaving a secure pensionable position. Think of it! A teacher! The first from the generations of plebs to which he belongs to make such breakthrough – to the professions! And going off without prospects, John-John, to God knows where!'

JUNIOR. To become a writer.

TOM. 'Others – youths!' –

JUNIOR. Taking to hard liquor – Wuw!

TOM. 'And all, it would appear, being influenced by something called the *vision* of a Johnny-come-lately.'

LIAM. That's right, fellas, JJ was a blow-in, a cute buff-sham from back there Caherlistrane-side.

TOM. 'Too far too fast for us, John-John.'

MICHAEL. And that was the warning?

TOM (*silent 'No'*). 'I think – John – you would be well advised to leave the decision-making to the parents and their spiritual advisors as to what is best for their children. I know you have it in you to take careful account of what I have said and the *security* of wiser steps.'

MICHAEL. That sounds more like a threat.

TOM. 'Holy Moses, Michael — John-John — we don't threaten anyone. We don't have to. We, the poor conservatives — troglodytes, if you will — have seen these little phases come and go. All we have to do is wait.'

MICHAEL *laughs. Then ritual toast:*

MICHAEL. Good luck!

TOM. 'God bless you.'

JUNIOR. Luck!

LIAM. Good luck, fellas!

MICHAEL. But he might show up.

TOM *shakes his head.*

Aw, you'd never know.

TOM *throws his head back at* MICHAEL's *romantic hope springing eternal.*

LIAM. Strangers wanting to run the town.

MICHAEL. There was never anything like it before. And where did that lousy partition come out of?

TOM *and* JUNIOR — *with no great interest — notice the partition for the first time.*

LIAM. No decent heating in the place. The place was mighty cold without that.

MICHAEL. And how is Silver Strand?

LIAM. Oh! Oh!

JUNIOR. Tell him.

LIAM. Aw no, fellas!

JUNIOR. Tell him! The place is crawling with priests and police since the bishop's niece got poled back there last year — Tell him.

LIAM. Well. Well. I shifted this Judy at a dance in Seapoint and wheeled her back to the Strand, and we were coorting away there nicely — No! No! A fair coort mind! I hadn't even bothered to let back the seats of the auld jalop. But next thing — suddenly — my heart was in my mouth. Tap-tap-tap at the window, and it all fogged up. A big policeman with a flashlamp. What are yeh doin' there, says he. Kneckin', fella, says I. Well, says he — Well, says he, stick your neck now back in your trousers and hump off.

They laugh.

JUNIOR. Tell him about Dooley.

TOM. Aw wait'll I tell yeh.

JUNIOR. Yeh remember Dooley?

MICHAEL. The librarian is it?

TOM. Shiny boots —

JUNIOR. Holy Harry —

TOM. First Mass, Communion, a pillar of the community. Well, it's all an act. He hates it all: Church, State, everything.

JUNIOR. Jasus, Jasus, Jasus . . .

TOM. Stall it a minute now. The headmaster sent me down to organise some kind of library service with him for the school and we got talking. And d'yeh know his great secret rebellion against it all? Called me down to the shelf like this. *The Life Story of the Little Flower* filed under horticulture. Well laugh when I saw it? I nearly died. And giggling away to himself. The malice! I never enjoyed anything so much. (*Laughter subsiding.*) Well yourself?

MICHAEL. Oh, having a great time. You know?

TOM. *News! News!*

MICHAEL. Well, I was with this buddy of mine one night and we picked up these two chicks in a bar.

LIAM. Yeh? –

JUNIOR. Yeh?

MICHAEL. Well. It was coming to closing time anyway and they're clearing the glasses away, see, and one of the barmen – just like that – grabbed the glass out of one of the chick's hands –

LIAM. Yeh? –

JUNIOR. Yeh?

MICHAEL. And this buddy of mine – and he's only a little guy – took a swing at the barman, and the barman – and not at my buddy – but a swing at the chick. So I took a swing at the barman. Me! You know?

TOM. Missed.

MICHAEL. Yeh. And then, the most marvellous choreographed movement, three more barmen vaulting over the counter and –

TOM. You all ended up on your arses outside.

MICHAEL. Yeh, and then –

TOM. You all had to go back meekly for your overcoats . . . You told us ten years ago!

MICHAEL. . . . Well, I was at this party the other night and I don't know what came over me, but I did something crazy.

TOM. Yeh?

LIAM. Yeh? –

JUNIOR. Yeh? –

TOM. Yeh?

MICHAEL (*evasive*). No, forget that. But, ah, forget that, I was in the Village – you know? – one of those Village bars there recently and –

TOM. No, the party the other night – you did something crazy – What were you going to say?

MICHAEL. Ah, that was nothing. But, one of those Village bars, and, and, listening to these two weirdos. One of them proving that Moses was in fact a stonecutter.

LIAM. Proving it?

MICHAEL. Proving it: dates, figures, blisters, the lot. And the other fella –

LIAM. The Ten Commandments?!

MICHAEL. The other fella trying to get in with his own thesis, 'Yeah, man, I dig, man, but do you believe Jesus Christ committed suicide?'

TOM. They're daft alright.

MICHAEL. It was very funny.

LIAM. And no one around to give one of them a box?

MICHAEL. It was very funny.

JUNIOR. Moses up the mountain chiselling away on the quiet behind a cloud.

MICHAEL. It was very funny, Junie.

JUNIOR. That's a good one.

But the general feeling is that it is not such a good one.

LIAM. But you're faring out well over there, Mick?

MICHAEL. Yep.

LIAM. Hah?

MICHAEL. Oh, pretty good. I'm – I'm up for this part in a film, actually. And that tele a while back. And there's a possibility of a part in a stage play, but we don't know yet.

TOM. 'We'? Who?

MICHAEL. My agent.

TOM. Oh, *you* have an agent?

MICHAEL. I had an agent the last time I was home, what's wrong with an agent?

TOM. I didn't say there was anything.

MICHAEL. Everyone has an agent.

JUNIOR. Begobs I haven't.

MICHAEL. I'd say averaging ten – eleven grand over the past two/three years. That's not bad.

JUNIOR. Not bad he says and the few quid a week my auld fella gives me.

MICHAEL. What? Well, it's not bad. It's not good either. I know guys making fifty – a hundred grand a year.

JUNIOR. I know fellas making nothing.

TOM. So what? What are you telling us for?

MICHAEL. Well, I wouldn't have made it clerking around here.

TOM. You wouldn't.

JUNIOR. Or teaching.

TOM. What are you laughing at? – You wouldn't, you can say that again.

JUNIOR (*laughing*). You could sing that, sir!

TOM. Tck, Jack!

JUNIOR (*guffawing*). As the bishop said to the actress!

TOM. Shut up, you eejit!

JUNIOR (*continues laughing/singing*). 'Sure no letter I'll be wearin', for soon will I be sailing –' (*To* MICHAEL.) Hey, did you bring any home with yeh?

Laughing subsiding.

MICHAEL. But I was in this place the other night.

TOM. The party, is it?

MICHAEL. No. Yes. But there was a guy there anyway –

TOM. Who?

MICHAEL. No, wait'll you hear this one, Tom. A fella, some nut, I didn't know him.

TOM. Yeh?

LIAM. Yeh? –

JUNIOR. Yeh? –

TOM. Yeh?

MICHAEL. Well, he went a bit berserk anyway.

JUNIOR. Beresk!

TOM. Shh!

MICHAEL. Well. He took off his clothes. (*He looks at them, unsure, his vulnerability showing; he is talking about himself.*) Well, he took off his clothes. Well, bollocks naked, jumping on tables and chairs, and then he started to shout 'No! No! This isn't it at all! This kind of – life – isn't it at all. Listen! Listen to me! Listen! I have something to tell you all!'

TOM. Making his protest.

MICHAEL. Yeh.

TOM. Yeh?

MICHAEL. Something to tell them all.

TOM. Yeh?

MICHAEL. Whatever – message – he had, for the world. But the words wouldn't come for him anyway. And (*Moment's pause; then, simply.*) Well. Then he tried to set himself on fire. (*He averts his eyes.*)

LIAM. Women there, Mick?

MICHAEL. Yeh. (*Mustering himself again.*) Ah, it wasn't anything serious – I mean, a party, a weirdo job. They were only laughing at him.

TOM. Yeh?

MICHAEL. Well, that's it. (*Forces a laugh.*) They calmed him down – put out the flames, what?

TOM. Yeh?

LIAM. Yeh?

MICHAEL. Oh yes! (*Trying to laugh.*) But then, then, one of the women took off *her* clothes and started cheering 'Up the Irish, up the IRA!'

TOM (*quietly*). His protest really foiled.

MICHAEL. Yeh.

LIAM. He was *Irish*?

MICHAEL. What?

JUNIOR. But what was up with him?

LIAM. He was *Irish*?

MICHAEL. Yeh.

JUNIOR. But what was up with him?

MICHAEL. I don't know. Maybe someone put something in his drink or – There were all sorts of things going round – I mean, we, *we* were only laughing at him.

LIAM. Did you know him, Mick?

MICHAEL. I mean, I was drunk out of my skull myself.

TOM. Yeh?

MICHAEL. Well, that's it. Then he started crying, put on his clothes, I suppose, and left. I thought it was a good one.

LIAM. Did you know him, Mick?

TOM. Well that's a good one.

Exchanges glances with JUNIOR.

JUNIOR. 'Tis.

MICHAEL. I thought it was a good one.

LIAM. Did he pull the quare one?

MICHAEL. What?

LIAM. The one that took off her clothes.

MICHAEL (*extreme reaction*). Aw for Jesus' sake, Liam!

LIAM. I was only joking.

TOM. Well that's a good one.

JUNIOR. 'Tis.

MICHAEL (*he goes to the counter*). We need another round.

PEGGY *has entered the front door and hallway. Now poking her head in lounge doorway. She is forty.*

PEGGY. Hello, did he arrive, is he here, did he come? Ary how yeh, Ridge, y'auld eejit yeh, you're as beautiful as ever, janeymack you're looking delicious, you're as welcome as the flowers in May!

MICHAEL. Peggy!

PEGGY. Look at you – gorgeous – and the suit!

MICHAEL. You're looking well.

PEGGY. Oh flattery, flattery! Holding my own –

MISSUS (*appearing for a moment to see who has arrived*).
Aaa –

PEGGY. How long are you home for?

MICHAEL. Oh –

MISSUS. Peggy –

PEGGY. How long? – Hello, Missus –

MICHAEL. Well –

PEGGY. A few weeks?

MICHAEL. Yeh. Well, we'll see.

PEGGY. Well you're a sight for sore eyes, you didn't change a bit, he's looking tip-top, isn't he?

TOM. Will you sit down –

PEGGY. Bejaneymack tonight, you're looking smashing!

TOM. Will you sit down and don't be making a show of yourself!

She sticks out her tongue at TOM, *pokes a finger in his ribs and sits on the arm of his chair, stroking his hair.*

TOM *making private world-weary faces to himself.*

PEGGY. When did you arrive?

MICHAEL. Last night.

PEGGY. Aa, did yeh?

MICHAEL. What are you having, Peggy.

PEGGY. Well, I'm going to have a gin and tonic in honour of yourself if his Nibs will allow me.

MICHAEL. Will we switch to shorts?

TOM. Oh? The Yank.

JUNIOR. The returned wank as the fella says!

MICHAEL (*calls*). The same again Missus, please!

TOM (*mock belligerently – as is his style*). I'll have a
   whiskey! –

JUNIOR. I'll stick to the pint –

LIAM. And a shot o' malt for me, Mike.

MICHAEL. Gin and tonic, Missus, three Scotch and a pint.

TOM. Irish!

MICHAEL. What?

TOM. Irish! Irish!

LIAM. And an Irish for me, Mike. Nothing but.

MICHAEL. One Scotch, Missus.

MISSUS. Thanks, thanks, alright, Michael.

PEGGY. Well.

   Short silence.

LIAM. 'Around the fire one winter's night the farmer's rosy
   children sat.'

TOM. Oh?

PEGGY. It's nice to see us all together again, isn't it, it's like old
   times?

TOM. Isn't there a chair over there for yeh!

JUNIOR (*vacating his chair*). Here, a girleen.

PEGGY (*tongue out at* TOM, *a finger in his ribs*). Sourpuss!
   (*And takes* JUNIOR's *chair.*)

JUNIOR (*belches*). Better out than your eye!

PEGGY. But tell us who you met over there, tell us all about the
   stars.

MICHAEL. Oh! (*Shrugs.*)

   TOM *sighs.*

PEGGY. Did you meet what's-his-name?

TOM (*to himself*). Tck!

MICHAEL. You meet them all different times.

TOM (*to himself*). Do yeh?

MICHAEL. Peter O'Toole.

PEGGY. Aa go on.

JUNIOR (*impressed*). Did yeh, did yeh though?

LIAM. Old Lawrence himself.

MICHAEL. Jack Lemmon.

PEGGY. And the other fella, the long fella?

MICHAEL. No.

JUNIOR. Did you ever meet –

MICHAEL. Paul Newman, Al Pacino.

PEGGY. Louis Jordan?

MICHAEL. Who?

TOM. Hopalong Cassidy. (*To* JUNIOR.) Give us a cigarette.

JUNIOR. That big one, the Redgrave one – Veronica, is it?

TOM (*irritably*). Vanessa.

JUNIOR. Fine bird – Oosh! Big.

TOM. You must be a very popular fella over there, Michael.

JUNIOR. You must be a very familiar fella over there, sir.

TOM (*groans*). Isn't this awful.

JUNIOR. Jealousy will get you nowhere, Ryan.

TOM. D'yeh hear Jack, D'yeh hear Sonny, off-to-Palestine
   head. Palestine, was it, or the Congo, was it, Junie, you were
   going to a few years ago?

JUNIOR. You were the one always talking about travelling – JJ arranging things for you – you were the one was meant to be off doing the great things.

TOM. I never mentioned the Palestine Police Force.

JUNIOR (*laughing – as is the case with the others through the following*). I got married.

TOM. And look at the cut of you!

JUNIOR. Nice home, nice baba, nice wife, Gloria – (*Singing.*) Oosh, she has a lovely bottom – set of teeth.

TOM. Ah but sure, what harm, your children will travel, your son will.

JUNIOR. He won't be a schoolmaster anyway.

TOM. An architect in Canada.

PEGGY (*laughing shrilly*). Oh yes, he was telling us one night!

TOM (*philosophical sniff*). But d'yeh see what I mean, the way the people are here; passing the buck. Twenty-seven years of age –

JUNIOR. Thirty-one –

TOM. And he's talking about what a five-month old son is going to do.

JUNIOR. Trotsky!

TOM. Now! That's smiling Jack the Palestine Policeman!

JUNIOR. Now! The great writer; did ye read his great socialist piece in *Boy's Own*?

TOM. Did you mend many carburettors today?

JUNIOR. Did yous give many slaps today?

He drains his glass; MISSUS is approaching with a tray of drinks. She serves LIAM first as usual.

MISSUS. Now, yas, that's the boy, Liam.

JUNIOR. Off to write his great book.

LIAM. Thank you, Mrs Kilkelly.

JUNIOR. But he had the first page wrote – the dedication, 'In gratitude to J.J. Kilkelly'.

TOM reacts to this but bides his time.

LIAM. A nation of drop-outs as that professor said on the Late Late Show.

MISSUS. When will be seeing you on television, Michael, we do be watching?

MICHAEL. Well, it's a question of whether the things I'm in are sold to here or –

But MISSUS is already on her way back to the bar.

MISSUS. Your pint is on the way, Junior.

JUNIOR. No hurry, Missus. (*Sighs, lamenting into his empty glass.*)

TOM. I never dedicated anything to anyone.

JUNIOR. You never wrote anything.

TOM. And I certainly never thought of dedicating anything to JJ.

JUNIOR. Off to travel round the world to gain experience, and look at him, lazier than Luke O'Brien's dog that has to lean up against the wall to bark.

Big laugh.

PEGGY. Well, cheers, Michael!

MICHAEL. Good health, Peggy!

JUNIOR. Cathaoireacha! (*Chairs*)

PEGGY (*to MICHAEL*). You're a tonic.

LIAM. Good luck, fellas!

PEGGY. You're just what we needed.

JUNIOR (*again to his glass*). Yas.

PEGGY. But tell us all.

MICHAEL. Oh. You know?

PEGGY. Aa go on now, tell us all.

TOM *groans*.

What's up with you tonight?

TOM. 'Tell us all.' What does that mean?

PEGGY *looks away, hurt*.

LIAM. The sooner you two mavericks get hitched, the better.

TOM. Did you hear the definition of the gentleman farmer? A fella who bulls his own cows.

LIAM (*through the laughter*). Ryan! . . . Ryan! One good heifer any day is worth two months of a teacher's salary pound for pound.

TOM. Sterling or avoirdupois, Liam?

Off, the town clock ringing nine.
MISSUS *approaching with* JUNIOR's *pint*.

LIAM. Ryan! Ryan! I made four hundred and twenty-eight pounds on a single deal last week.

TOM. At a puffed up auction.

JUNIOR. God bless yeh, Missus.

LIAM. What?

TOM. Nothing. Good man.

MISSUS. Now.

MICHAEL *has risen to pay for the round but* LIAM *is now awkwardly on his feet, bumping into* JUNIOR, *in his haste.*

LIAM. No! No! It's my round! I'm getting this! –

JUNIOR (*protecting his pint*). Jasus! –

MICHAEL. This one is mine, Liam –

LIAM. No! No! Don't take anyone's money!

TOM. He's getting carried away.

LIAM. My round, fella! –

MISSUS. Sure it's alright, Liam. –

LIAM (*to* MICHAEL). I've a question for you in a minute –

MISSUS. Sure it's –

LIAM. No! And have one yourself, Mrs Kilkelly.

MISSUS. No thanks, Liam, you're too good. (*Returning to bar.*)

LIAM. As a matter of fact my salary last year was – Well, it was in excess – greatly in excess of any figure you mentioned, boy. How much tax did you pay last year?

TOM. Sit down! –

LIAM. How much? –

JUNIOR. Sit *down*! –

LIAM. For a little comparison, boy –

TOM. Sit down outa that! –

JUNIOR. For Jasus' sake! Good luck who stood!

MISSUS *returning with change for* LIAM.

MISSUS. Now, Liam. That's the man.

PEGGY. How's the lodger, Missus?

JUNIOR. Josephine, wuw!

MISSUS *laughs, catering for them.*

PEGGY (*aside to* MICHAEL). Were they telling you about the one?

MISSUS. Aa but she's nice.

JUNIOR. Very good-natured they say.

MISSUS. But talking to the lads and her tea waiting on her in there this two hours. (*Wandering out to front door.*) That's who I am waiting for now. (*Alone in front door.*) D'ye know now. (*Where she remains for some moments.*)

Off, the church clock is chiming nine.

PEGGY. The place is gone to hell, isn't it?

MICHAEL. I don't know. Not irreparably. But *who* put up that partition? This was all one room. Remember, Tom, one of your socialist ideas to JJ? We were all very impressed: that there should be no public bar, no divisions or class distinctions.

LIAM. What d'yeh mean, not irreparably, fella?

MICHAEL (*not listening*). What? Get rid of that (*partition*) and see the space we'd have.

LIAM. I wouldn't like to be the fella to inherit the debts of this place.

MICHAEL. What are you on about all evening, Liam?

LIAM. You're not fond of America, Mick?

MICHAEL. This was our roots, Liam. This was to be our continuing cultural cradle: 'Let the word go forth from this time and place —' What? We could do it again! Wake up, wake up, boys and girls! — 'with a constant flow of good ideas.'

TOM *laughs/snorts at* MICHAEL's *romanticism.*

What?

JUNIOR. We could!

TOM. Oh God, two of ye!

MICHAEL. But doesn't it seem a pity?

LIAM. That's okay, Mick –

MICHAEL. Well, doesn't it?

TOM. Create another pub?

MICHAEL. It was more than a pub.

TOM. Our culture, as indeed our nationalism, has always had the profoundest connections with the pub.

LIAM. That's okay, fella. I'm keeping my eye on it quietly. I've the customer already on my books that it suits.

PEGGY. Now. And poor Missus has other ideas. She thinks she has him earmarked for Anne.

LIAM (*cockily – and he is drunker than the others*). I'm in no hurry for any Anne, or any other Anne (*To* MICHAEL.) And, fella – fella! – that partition, out of the goodness of my pocket and my heart. Without obligation.

MICHAEL *looks at* TOM. TOM *has been waiting for him.*

TOM (*blandly*). Yeh?

LIAM (*laughs*). Unless, of course, you or your agent or your dollars would like me to handle the purchase for you. (*Sings in celebration to himself.*) 'Put the blanket on the ground!' (*And drinks.*)

MICHAEL *looks at* TOM *again.*

TOM (*smiles blandly*). The torch has been passed to a new generation.

JUNIOR (*has been puzzling over a song to himself*). 'The Sheep with their little lambs, passed me by on the road' – How does that begin?

TOM (*still smiling blandly, cynically at* MICHAEL). Hmm?

JUNIOR. That was JJ's song.

MICHAEL. But. (*Drinks.*) No, but, Annette, come to think of it now, she looks like JJ.

PEGGY. Aa did you meet her? Isn't she a dote?

TOM. That's an extraordinary observation, Michael, seeing you didn't recognise her when you saw her.

MICHAEL. Aw, she does, does, looks like JJ.

PEGGY. But what has you home at this awful time of the year?

TOM. Hope, refuge, to drink from his wellsprings, the romantic in his fancy suit.

MICHAEL. It'd be no harm if you smartened yourself up a bit.

TOM (*going to counter*). You'll have to do better than that. Missus! Give us a packet of cigarettes. Ten Carrolls.

JUNIOR (*still trying to work it out*). 'The sheep with their little lambs passed me on the road.'

MICHAEL. What's your news, Peggy, they told me nothing.

PEGGY. Did they tell you we have a new priest?

MICHAEL. No. What's he like?

TOM. Ridiculous. Jesus, the last fella was bad, Fr. Connolly was a snob, but at least that's something: this fella is an eejit.

PEGGY. For as much as you see of the church to know what he is.

TOM. Ah, but I went to check him out. My dear brethren – This was his sermon one Sunday. (*A warning to* PEGGY!) Don't interrupt me now. A maan (*man*) wan time, wan place, somewhere, that kept leaving the church before the maas (*Mass*) was ended, and continued this maalpractice though repeatedly warned about it. An' wan Sunday, my dear brethern, wasn't he sloping outa the church wance again, an' just as he was stepping outside didn't he look up at the clock to see what time 'twas, and d'yeh know what happened to

him? – d'ye know what happened to him! The church clock
fell off the tower on top of him. Now! Killed stone dead.

PEGGY. Oh that's exaggerated, love.

TOM. Ridiculous. In this day and age! And the young ones are
worse, falling over backwards, arse over elbow, to talk about
sex to show how progressive they are. Sex: progressive –
Jesus! – Ridiculous – Smoke? (*To* JUNIOR.)

PEGGY. You never see any good in the Church.

TOM. Aa but I do, love. Look at Liam there, and he's a regular
churchgoer. And think of how the marriage figures all over
the country would have slumped again only for all the young
nuns jumping over the wall and the young priests waiting for
them outside with their cassocks lifted.

PEGGY. Oh that's not right.

TOM. Ridiculous. Tell us something, Ridge, anything,
something interesting, for God's sake.

PEGGY. . . . You got quiet or something, Michael. Tell us how
are all the girls treating you? Oh, there was a rumour some
time back – Wasn't there, love? – that you were married?

MICHAEL. No.

PEGGY. What?

MICHAEL. I answered that one.

PEGGY. What?

MICHAEL. Well, there was a girl – some time back. I knew her
quite well – intimately – know what I mean? She was
working in this night club, and this guy starts chatting her up,
charming her, et cetera.

LIAM. Yeh?

JUNIOR. Big bird?

MICHAEL. But this guy, he had a few bucks anyway, a yacht and all that, and he was trying to persuade her go off on a trip with him.

JUNIOR. Yi-yi!

MICHAEL. That's the point. Eventually she did, the two of them alone on the boat for three weeks and he never tried to make her, never laid a hand on her. And she committed suicide.

TOM. Ary Ridge!

MICHAEL. I thought that would be your reaction.

LIAM. What?

TOM. Tck!

PEGGY (*smiling/frowning*). Did she drown herself or what Michael?

LIAM. A good boot in the arse she wanted.

MICHAEL. He was a sadist or something.

JUNIOR. He was a gomey if you ask me.

TOM. And what's to signify in that story?

MICHAEL. I knew her. She was – a friend. And I knew him.

TOM (*rising*). Ridiculous country. The luck is on me I never left here. (*Calls.*) You might as well start filling the acthoring man's round, Missus!

MICHAEL. Better make them doubles!

TOM. Oh?

MICHAEL. Some people need the stimulation.

TOM *laughs and exits to the Gents.*

PEGGY. But you must go into a lot of queer places over there?

MICHAEL. Maybe they'd only be *queer* to people from round here.

MISSUS. Doubles, Michael?

MICHAEL. Yes! Why not!

PEGGY. Oh, did they tell you they nearly marched on the North one night?

MISSUS. And a pint for you, Junior?

JUNIOR. Aye-aye, Missus!

PEGGY. Did they tell you?

LIAM. You're not a political animal, Mike?

MICHAEL. Excuse me, Liam, but no one round here ever called me Mick, Mike or Mickeen, okay?

LIAM *nods, gravely bovine.*
MICHAEL *offering cigarettes around.*
PEGGY *accepts one unconsciously.*
JUNIOR *singing snatches of 'All in the April Evening'.*

PEGGY. But you're getting on well over there?

MICHAEL. Strugglin'. Smoke, Junie?

PEGGY. Aa go on, but are –

JUNIOR. Thanks boy –

PEGGY. But are yeh getting on well though?

MICHAEL. Yep.

LIAM. Never use 'em.

PEGGY. But seriously, are you? (*He is lighting her cigarette.*)

MICHAEL. Yes.

JUNIOR ⎱ 'The sheep with their little lambs . . .'
PEGGY ⎰ Oh I didn't want this at all.

(*But she puffs away at it.*) But do yeh like it all the time?

MICHAEL (*irritably*). Yes, Peggy, it's marvellous.

PEGGY. I see.

MICHAEL. And how are things with you?

PEGGY. Oh now.

MICHAEL. What?

PEGGY. Oh indeed –

MICHAEL. Yes?

PEGGY. Oh now, don't ask me.

MICHAEL. You gave up the dressmaking, didn't you?

PEGGY. Well, yeh know, around here.

MICHAEL. And the singing?

PEGGY. What singing? (*Remembering, laughing shrilly.*) Oh
yes! JJ and his classical music, and he having me up to the
nuns taking singing lessons. Wasn't I the eejit? And wait'll I
tell yeh. (*Whispering.*) I had a crush on him. That slob. And
he old enough to be my father. I'm not saying anything, it
was all in innocence. And Sister Jerome, the singing teacher,
tone deaf.

JUNIOR ⎱ 'Passed me by on the road.'
MICHAEL ⎰ Who was the slob?

PEGGY. JJ! Wait'll Tom comes back. (*He'll tell you*).

MICHAEL. So, you're minding the house with your mother?

PEGGY. Oh but I do a morning or two a week, now and again,
bookkeeping for the vet.

MICHAEL. And how is that old friend of yours, Helen Collins?

PEGGY. Isn't she married? Sure you must have known – She's producing like mad. Well, three and one on the way, as they say. But she's let herself go to hell – Hasn't she, Junie? – I'm meant to look like her daughter and she's ten months younger than me.

MICHAEL. I see.

PEGGY. But sure you must have known, wasn't she an old flame of yours? (*She pauses for only the briefest moment not wanting to acknowledge the thought that he has been getting at her.*) Oh but they're hopefully going to open a tourist office here next year – isn't that right, Liam? – and I'm in the running for it (*A smile at* LIAM.) if I know the right people. (*Then smiling bravely, a glance at* MICHAEL, *then averts her eyes.* MICHAEL *feeling ashamed of himself, looks at her empty glass and his own.*)

MICHAEL. That's – That's great. Hang on.

He goes to the counter and returns with his own and PEGGY's *drink.*

LIAM. An' so was Beethoven, fellas. Stone deaf.

MICHAEL (*toasting* PEGGY). The best! Those curtains are yours.

PEGGY. And I was up all night finishing them. And never got paid.

MICHAEL. We didn't want to get paid.

PEGGY (*impulsively, she throws her arms around him*). Ary, yeh daft and romantic, it's lovely to see yeh! Oh gosh-golly, this is gone out again.

MICHAEL relights her cigarette.
MISSUS approaching with TOM's *and* LIAM's *drinks.*

MISSUS. I'll clear a few of these glasses out of yer way now.

JUNIOR. And the pint, Missus?

MISSUS. That's coming, Junior.

JUNIOR *sighs to himself*.

PEGGY. And d'yeh know? I could whistle the whole of the Sixth Symphony from beginning to end.

TOM (*returning from Gents*). They're daft alright.

PEGGY. Stop now, we were having a lovely time while you were out.

TOM. But do you yourself take questions like that seriously now?

PEGGY. Cheers, Michael!

MICHAEL. Cheers!

LIAM. Luck, fellas!

TOM. Michael?

MICHAEL. Questions like what?

LIAM. Questions like did Jesus Ch – Did you-know-who commit suicide.

TOM. And questions of the immoral and unethical behaviour of not screwing a bird on a boat.

MISSUS *returning to the bar*.

And, as Liam so delicately put it, for the proprietress's and my fiancée's sensitivities no doubt, questions like do you believe did you-know-who commit suicide.

MICHAEL. What's up with you?

TOM (*philosophical sniff*). Aw now.

JUNIOR (*to himself*). Aw fuck this! – Missus! – (*Striding to the bar, frustrated by his empty glass.*) Give me a drop of the hard tack too, and as well as the pint you're filling *now* you might start filling *another* pint for whoever is buying the next round.

MICHAEL. What's up with you?

TOM. Aw now.

PEGGY. You've changed, Michael.

MICHAEL. *I've* changed?

PEGGY. You used to be a grand shy lad with just the odd old, yeh know, flourish.

TOM. And supercilious with it.

MICHAEL. Well, I never nearly marched on the North, and I never thought a bank clerk is any more ridiculous for what she does than anybody else, and I never thought the jackboot in the arse was the cure for everything, and I never thought –

LIAM. Hold it, fella –

MICHAEL. That you (*Tom*) did either –

LIAM. Right there, fella –

MICHAEL. And to think of it! –

LIAM. Fella! –

MICHAEL. We were going to change all this!

LIAM. Fella!

TOM. You're missing the point –

MICHAEL. In this very room! And now it's bollocks talk about Protestants –

TOM. No one said anything about –

MICHAEL. The great anti-cleric (*Tom*) nearly going off to fight a Holy War!

TOM. No one said anything about –

LIAM. A minority Catholic group being oppressed! –

MICHAEL. You must be very unhappy in your lives –

TOM. Nothing to do with clerics –

LIAM. Fella! –

TOM. It's your ridiculous attitude –

LIAM. Brave Irish Catholic men and women –

MICHAEL. Everything seems ridiculous to you –

TOM. Women and sex orgies and some myth in your mind about JJ –

LIAM. Because – because a discriminating majority –

MICHAEL. You're really into 1917 –

TOM. What's all this talk about JJ? –

LIAM. A discriminating and – And! – gerrymandering majority! –

MICHAEL. Back to the stuck-in-the-mud-festering ignorance! –

TOM. 'Wellsprings and lost horizons!' –

MICHAEL. Yes! –

LIAM. A gerrymandering! –

MICHAEL. Lost horizons! –

LIAM. Fella, fella! A gerrymandering majority! –

TOM. Never arriving at reality –

LIAM. You can't deny it, you can't deny it – And! –

TOM. All mixed up –

LIAM. And! Racial memory, boy! –

TOM. Stop, Liam –

LIAM. Deny that one, boy! –

TOM. Stop, Liam! –

LIAM. Cause you can't deny it! – And! – And! – You can't deny it! –

TOM. Stop! –

LIAM. Cause – cause! – Fella! – Fella! –

TOM. Stop-stop-stop!

LIAM. You can't deny it!

TOM. Stop, will you, Liam! – Stop! – Forget that.

LIAM. I will not forget it! (*Forgetting it.*) I will not forget it.

TOM. You and your kind with your rose-coloured lights that you can switch on and off so easily. You don't want reality.

MICHAEL. Well, if yours is the reality.

TOM. Oh?

MICHAEL. Reality is always about poverty, is it?

TOM. No, it's always about flowers. Look, excuse me, Michael –

But LIAM *is off again.*

LIAM. And there's a thing called Truth, fella – you may not have heard of it. And Faith, fella. And Truth and Faith and Faith and Truth inex – inextricably – inextricably bound. And-And! – cultural heritage – you may not (have) heard of it – No border, boy! And cultural heritage inex-inextricably bound with our Faith and Hope and Hope and Faith and *Truth*! And some of us, and some of us, at least, cherish and – cherish and – and – are not supercilious, boy, with it – about it. Fella! I will not forget it! Last refuge in Europe.

TOM. Fine, Liam. Rest yourself now.

JUNIOR (*in answer to a glance from* LIAM). Well spoken, boy.

TOM. Look, excuse me, Michael, but what is the point, the real issue of what we are discussing!

MICHAEL. Well, maybe I have changed, because my enjoyment in life comes from other things than recognising my own petty malice in others.

TOM. Is that the point?

MICHAEL. A simple matter – and it's not a dream – of getting together and doing what we did before.

TOM. Is that the point? To do what we did before? And tell me, what did we do before?

MICHAEL. To do what we did before!

TOM (to himself). Jesus! Extraordinary how the daft romantics look back at things.

MICHAEL. Why is everyone calling me a romantic?

TOM. It's more polite.

MICHAEL. You would never have made the statements you are making tonight a few years ago.

LIAM. I'd reckon, fella, that proves he ain't static.

MICHAEL. It depends on which direction he went.

LIAM. I'd reckon, fella, that you are all – (washed-up).

TOM. No. Hold on. I think you're serious, Michael, hmm? I think he's serious. I think we have another leader. Another true progressive on our hands at last, lads. Another white fuckin' liberal.

PEGGY. Shh, love!

TOM. Home to re-inspire us, take a look at our problems, shake us out of our lethargy, stop us vegetating, show us where we went wrong –

MICHAEL. You're choosing the words –

TOM. Show us that we're not forgotten, bringing his new suicidal fuckin' Christ with him!

PEGGY. Love –

MICHAEL. Vegetating, lathargy, forgotten –

TOM. And most surprisingly, I think the poor hoor – like his illustrious predecessor – does not know where he is himself.

MICHAEL (*laughs*). I've been having a great time –

TOM. No! – No! –

MICHAEL. Marvellous time!

TOM. You're too depressed, Jack, too much on the defensive Jack –

MICHAEL. Marvellous! But cheers anyway, Jack, cheers!

TOM. The point, Michael, the real point and issue for you, Michael – D'yeh want to hear? You came home to stay, to *die*, Michael.

LIAM. Correct.

TOM. And fair enough, do that, but be warned, we don't want another JJ.

MICHAEL (*laugh/smile is gone*). I never mentioned I had any intention of staying home.

LIAM. Correct.

MICHAEL. What do you know about JJ?

LIAM. Enough, fella. But leave it to me. I'll rescue this place shortly.

MICHAEL. You spent so much of your time away as a student, the story was they were going to build a house for you in the university.

TOM. Michael.

MICHAEL. And you know nothing about JJ either.

TOM. I'm marking your card for you. JJ is a slob.

MICHAEL. He –

TOM. A slob –

MICHAEL. Isn't.

TOM. Is, was, always will be. A slob. He's probably crying and slobbering on somebody's shoulder now this minute, somewhere around Galway. Missus in there treats him as if he were a child.

JUNIOR (*angrily, rising*). And what else can the woman do?

TOM. I'm just telling him.

JUNIOR (*exits to Gents*). Jesus!

MICHAEL. Why?

TOM. Why what?

MICHAEL. Why are you telling me – and glorying in it?

TOM. JJ is a *dangerous* and weak slob. He limped back from England, about 1960. England was finished for him. He could not face it again. I hope this is not ringing too many bells for you personally. And he would have died from drink, or *other* things, but for the fact that the John F. Kennedy show had started on the road round about then, and some auld women in the town pointed out doesn't he look like John F. Kennedy. And JJ hopped up on that American-wrapped bandwagon of so-called idealism –

MICHAEL. He had his own idealism.

TOM. Until he began to think he *was* John F. Kennedy.

MICHAEL. And, in a way, he was.

TOM. And Danny O'Toole up the road thinks he's Robert Mitchum and he only five feet two?

MICHAEL. He re-energised this whole town.

TOM. And Danny O'Toole is winning the west for us? Then people started to look at our new slob-hero afresh. People like Missus in there – she pinned her hopes on him – and, he quickly hopped up on her too. And, so, became the possessor of her premises, which we, and others, put together for him, restyled at his dictates into a Camelot, i.e., a thriving business for selling pints.

MICHAEL. No –

TOM. Alright, selling pints was a secondary consideration. Like all camelot-pub owners he would have welcomed a clientele of teetotallers. His real purpose of course was to foster the arts, to give new life to broken dreams and the – horn – of immortality, nightly, to mortal men . . . But then came the fall.

MICHAEL. The assassination.

TOM. Of whom?

MICHAEL. Kennedy.

TOM. Oh, I thought for a minute there you were talking about *our* president, JJ.

MICHAEL. Well.

TOM. What?

MICHAEL. Well, as I heard it, after Kennedy's death, the *character*-assassination of JJ started in earnest.

TOM. No.

MICHAEL. Well, as you said yourself earlier, the priest's visits, other people's visits and the people the priest represented.

TOM. No. After Kennedy's assassination, the grief, yes. We all experienced it. But is grief a life-long profession?

MICHAEL. A lot of people feared and hated JJ in this town.

TOM. Feared? No. Never.

MICHAEL. Well, even on the evidence of tonight one could easily get the impression that this town could have had a few things – just a few, Tom? – to do with 'our' president's fall.

TOM. No! Look, he hopped up on the load of American straw and he had so little going for him that when that load of straw went up in smoke, JJ went up with it. Oh yes, they *hated* him — Why wouldn't they: Puppetry, mimicry, rhetoric! What had he to offer anyone? Where were the facts, the definitions?

MICHAEL. Why are you getting so excited?

TOM. I'm not getting excited. He-fed-people's-fantasies. That all he did. Fed — people's — fantasies.

MICHAEL. People are afraid of realising themselves.

TOM. Look, look, look — lookit! (*To himself.*) Shit!

MICHAEL. They fear that.

TOM. Realising themselves? Like you did? Look! — Lookit! — leaving aside the superficial fact that he looked like John F. Kennedy — somewhere around the left ball — he could just as easily have thought he was John McCormack or Pope John. He had so little going for him and we are such a ridiculous race that even our choice of assumed images is quite arbitrary.

MICHAEL. Are you finished?

TOM. The only mercy in the whole business, as I see it, is that he did not in fact think he was John McCormack.

LIAM. Man, Tomeen!

MICHAEL. JJ's respect, opinion and esteem for you —

TOM. To thine own self be true? God we're a glorious people alright.

LIAM. C'rrect.

LIAM *has risen and is going to Gents.*

TOM. Look, don't fret yourself about not seeing him tonight —

MICHAEL. I haven't given up on seeing him tonight.

TOM (*groans*). Aw Lord! There are plenty of JJs about.
(*Pointing at* LIAM *who is exiting to Gents:*) I prefer *that*.

MICHAEL. You won't listen to my interpretation?

PEGGY. Aa, lads –

TOM. By all means – if you have one.

MICHAEL. JJ's opinion of you –

TOM. And if it's a sensible one.

MICHAEL. The *esteem* he held you in, always, way above the
   rest of us –

TOM. Ah-ah-ah-ah! Don't try that one. Remember where you
   are now. It's clear from the way you've been talking all night
   that the – innocence – naiveté of New York has softened your
   head, but remember you're talking to the people of a little
   town in the west of Ireland now: a little more sophisticated
   than that for us, Michael.

MICHAEL. JJ and his wife, his first wife, were walking along a
   street, and –

TOM. In England?

MICHAEL. Yes.

PEGGY. Lads.

TOM. Just making sure I'm following facts.

MICHAEL. And a car came along, the steering was perfect, the
   driver was sober, but the driver was some poor unhappy
   bitter little prick who wanted to kill someone, anyone, and he
   drove the car up on the footpath and knocked JJ's wife over,
   and she died in hospital three months later.

TOM. Yes.

MICHAEL. And that's what you describe as the *limp* JJ came into this town with?

TOM. Yes?

MICHAEL. What do you mean 'yes'?

TOM. Yes, I heard that story, and I'm sorry for him – if it's true.

MICHAEL. What?

TOM. No-no-no. Like, there are a lot of things we heard and believed some years ago, but we're a little older now.

MICHAEL. A man – after a tragedy like that –

TOM. More interesting stories are emerging about JJ's past.

MICHAEL. To pull himself together after a tragedy like that and start afresh.

TOM. Look, I don't recall anybody ever reading any headlines about that tragic and dramatic event.

PEGGY. He made it up, Michael.

TOM (*to* PEGGY). Keep out of it. And people are now of the opinion that JJ was never married before, that there was no first wife, that there was only a bird, and there was no –

MICHAEL. Jesus, you're exceeding yourself! What's happened to you?

TOM. Alright, there *was* an accident! – and you can drag your own limp into it and your own grandmother as well – but it does not change the fact of the point we are *now* discussing, which is that JJ is, was, always will be a slob. Now, can-you-contradict-me?

MICHAEL. I like him.

TOM. A-a-a-w! Back to the flowers. How nice, how fey, how easy for you! 'I like him.' And the way he upset and thwarted and wilfully and irresponsibly inflated and abused people. When I think of it. 'Together let us explore the stars.' Jesus!

JUNIOR *comes out of the Gents: his hand up for attention: he had got the first line of the song.*

JUNIOR. I've got it! 'All in the April evening'.

TOM (*to himself*). And left them high and dry.

PEGGY (*catering for him*). And bills outstanding all over the country, love, didn't he?

An angry grimace/gesture from TOM: *he does not want her comments. Junior – this is not his game – goes to the bar and stays there for some moments.*

JUNIOR. Missus! Throw us out that other pint.

TOM. God, we're a glorious people alright. Half of us, gullible eejits, people like yourself, ready to believe in anything. And the other half of us –

MICHAEL. People like yourself, ready to believe nothing.

TOM. People like yourself – people like yourself – ready to believe, get excited, follow to the death any old bollocks with a borrowed image, any old JJ who has read a book on American politics or business methods. Jesus, images: fuckin' neon shadows!

PEGGY. Love.

MICHAEL. And the other half of us ready to believe in nothing.

TOM. No! You don't understand! Never the sound, decent, honest-to-God man for us. Never again in this world, for us, or for anyone else.

JUNIOR *joins them.*

JUNIOR. Good luck, fellas.

Silence.

MICHAEL (*quietly*). He nearly made it.

TOM. 'Nearly'? I thought you were knocking us for that word a few minutes ago.

MICHAEL. He was great.

TOM. In what way? When? – How? – Where? – Convince me! – Tell me!

MICHAEL. He hadn't got over the first knock when the second happened.

TOM. Isn't that my proof, isn't that the test of a man? Sure all you're mentioning is his – dubious – misfortunes and some kind of hypothetical potential. What did he achieve? What was he talking about?

MICHAEL. I don't know what he was talking about but wasn't he right?

TOM. Tck! . . . That's fine, you don't know, that concludes the matter.

MICHAEL. Did you believe too much in him?

TOM. Now, I like that. You're coming up to our standards after all.

MICHAEL. Do you feel he let you down personally or what?

TOM. The gentle romantic has his subtly nasty side.

MICHAEL. Did you hope too much in him? – Was he your only lifeline?

TOM. No, I didn't hope too much in him, and I never ran messages for him or fell flat on my face for him.

MICHAEL. He didn't ask you to –

TOM. Bloody sure he didn't.

MICHAEL. Because you were the – doyen? – of his group.

TOM. I wouldn't have minded him – succeeding – but I had him taped from the start.

JUNIOR (*warning that* MISSUS *has appeared*). Yas, enough dialectics as the fella said.

But MISSUS *has come outside the bar-counter to intercept* LIAM *who is entering from the Gents and slip him a drink on the house and have a fawning word with him.*

TOM. I can see you're not the wide-eyed boy who left here –

MICHAEL. Thanks –

TOM. But since you have nothing to offer but a few distorted memories, and a few personal tricks on the burning monk caper, I'm marking your card. You've come home to stay, die, whatever – and you're welcome – but save us the bullshit. We've had that from your predecessor. We won't put up with it again. Don't try to emulate him, no re-energising, cultural cradles or stirring that old pot. Now I know you have it in you to take careful account of what I've said, and the *security* – Michael! – of wiser steps.

MICHAEL. Are you threatening me?

TOM. Holy Moses, Michael! – Me twin! – We don't threaten anyone. We don't have to! All we have to do – all we have ever had to do – is wait! (*He laughs.*) We leave it at that? God bless you.

MICHAEL. I'm not sure what I came home for, but I think I'm finding out.

LIAM *and* MISSUS *joining them.*

LIAM. Leave that matter to me, Mrs Kilkelly.

MISSUS. Better looking this man (LIAM) is getting every day, isn't he? D'ye know now. Yas. You didn't bring a blondie home with you, Michael?

MICHAEL. There are dark-haired girls in America too, Missus.

MISSUS. Musha, God help them. Be careful of them American ladies, a mac (*son*).

MICHAEL (*pointedly looking about*). How's business, Missus?

MISSUS. Oh, well, now, the off-season. Isn't that it, Liam?

LIAM. That is c'rrect, Mrs Kilkelly.

MISSUS. And things'll be picking up for us soon. Now.

MICHAEL. What you should do is get in a few of the natives telling funny stories for the tourists, and singing. And when things get going you could move out with the family and live in the henhouse for the season.

MISSUS. Isn't that what they're doing, some of them, living with the hens, to make room for tourists. And some of them, Michael —

MICHAEL. Yes, I didn't pay you for the last round.

MICHAEL *is standing, a roll of money ostentatiously in his hand. MISSUS feels offended by his cutting her short.*

MISSUS. Five pounds and sixty-nine new pence. Yas, your mother is delighted; I was talking to her for a minute this morning in the post office and she drawing out a wad of money. (*All get the implications of her remark. She gives MICHAEL change out of her cardigan pocket.*) Thanks, Michael. That's the woman with the money.

JUNIOR. Looking for a girl he is, Missus, wasn't he admiring the daughter?

MISSUS. Aa, Annette.

PEGGY. Aa, she's a dote! What's she going to do, Missus?

JUNIOR. I bet she wants to be an air hostess.

MISSUS. The cute Junior: how did you know that now?

JUNIOR. Oh-oh!

MISSUS. No. We were thinking of the bank. (*A glance at* LIAM.) Well, for the meanwhile, that is.

JUNIOR. Speak of an angel!

PEGGY. Oh hello, Anne!

ANNE (*silently*). Hello!

ANNE has come in. She moves aside with MISSUS to report briefly in a whisper – little more than a shake of her head. (She has not found her father) MISSUS *contains a sigh.*

PEGGY. The lovely coat! (Anne's)

MISSUS. And any sign of Josephine?

ANNE. She's up in Daly's lounge. She said she had a sandwich and not to bother with her tea.

MISSUS. Alright.

MISSUS wanders off, out to the front door, sighs out at the night, then exits upstairs. And, meanwhile, ANNE is taking off her coat and moving to attend the bar.

TOM. Anne! Come 'ere a minute. D'yeh know our acthoring man, Michael Ridge?

MICHAEL. D'yeh not remember me?

She has a natural shyness but it does not efface an interest she has in him.

Hmm?

ANNE. I do.

MICHAEL. What?

ANNE. I remember you here with Daddy.

MICHAEL. How is he?

ANNE. Not so good. (*She looks up at him, gravely, simply, for his reaction. He nods, simply, his understanding. Then she smiles.*) You're welcome home. (*And they shake hands.*)

TOM. Gee, kid, you were only so high when I saw you last.

MICHAEL. Is it Anne or Annette?

She shrugs: her gesture meaning that the choice is his.

Anne.

She nods, smiles, a silent 'okay'.

You're finished school?

ANNE. Three months time.

MICHAEL. And you won't be sorry.

ANNE. No. (*And she laughs.*)

PEGGY. Dreadful people, the nuns. Dreadful. Sister Bartholomew is the worst, don't you think, Anne?

ANNE. Isn't she dead?

PEGGY (*laughing shrilly*). Oh God yes, I forgot! I'm awful. But they're dreadful tyrants.

ANNE is already moving away.

MICHAEL. Will you come back and join us?

ANNE (*a toss of her head, smiling back at him*). I might.

TOM. Is it Anne or Annette, Michael?

MICHAEL. And she *is* like JJ. Well, things are looking up!

JUNIOR. Well we go up and have a few in Paddy Joe Daly's!

MICHAEL. The opposition, the enemy? No! We're grand here now.

JUNIOR. We'll introduce you to Josephine –

TOM ⎤ Grrrah!
JUNIOR ⎦ Grrrah!

PEGGY. But were they telling you about the one? And the hair? And the walk?

MICHAEL. Red hair? Frizzed out? I saw her crossing the street near the bank when I was driving my mother today.

PEGGY. The most ridiculous thing that ever hit this town – isn't she, love?

MICHAEL. I was wondering who she was. She's a fine-looking bird.

JUNIOR (*his appreciation again for large ladies*). She's big.

PEGGY. Excuse me –

JUNIOR. No bother there, sham.

MICHAEL. No! Anne! Hope!

TOM. God!

PEGGY. Excuse me! That girl (*Josephine*) is a fine looking?

MICHAEL. Hmm?

PEGGY. I'm disappointed in you, Michael.

LIAM. Dirty aul' thing.

JUNIOR. I hear she fancies you, cowboy.

PEGGY (*at* MICHAEL). Tck!

MICHAEL. What?

PEGGY. Your taste. That girl.

MICHAEL. I'm not interested in her.

TOM. Gee, tough luck on Josephine.

PEGGY (*neurotically*). She's a disgusting girl, she's stupid – Did you see her neck?

MICHAEL. I only said –

PEGGY. Of course you didn't. Everyone is talking about her, she won't last long here. She wouldn't even be kept in this place only for it's up to its eyes in debt.

TOM. What's up with yeh?

PEGGY. Every man in the town, married and single, around her, like – like terriers.

TOM. What's up with yeh?

PEGGY. Ary I get sick of this marvellous stuff. Everything is *marvellous* with Ridge.

MICHAEL. I only said –

PEGGY. Everything is *marvellous* –

MICHAEL. Alright she isn't marvellous –

PEGGY. Everything is *marvellous* –

TOM. What are ye – what's –

MICHAEL. But she's good-looking, good legs.

PEGGY. Everything is *marvellous* –

JUNIOR. Jugs (*tits*) –

MICHAEL. She has a good job –

JUNIOR. Bottom –

PEGGY. Will she keep it – Will she keep it? –

MICHAEL. Sexy-looking –

PEGGY. I don't agree, I don't agree! –

TOM. Wait a minute –

PEGGY. I don't agree! –

TOM. Hold on a minute –

PEGGY. Why should I agree? –

TOM. What are ye talking about! –

LIAM. She's a dirty aul' thing!

TOM (*silencing them*). What-are-ye-on-about! (*To* PEGGY.)
And what are you squealin' about?

PEGGY (*laughs suddenly, shrilly*). Ary shut up the lot of ye!

TOM. Are you finished? She's ridiculous alright.

PEGGY. Of course, she is –

TOM. And you're worse! The whole town is filled with –
pookies.

LIAM. Strangers comin' in to run the town, fellas.

TOM (*groans to himself, then*). Anne! Annette! Missus! Where
are they? Pint, gin, tonic, Scotch, two Irish! (*He feels*
MICHAEL's *eyes on him:*) Yeh?

MICHAEL. Why don't you leave?

TOM. But I might lose my religion.

PEGGY. What's he (*Michael*) saying?

MICHAEL. You can still get out.

TOM. But what of my unfinished work here? My feverish social
writings. Whose red pen would in merit and logic stand up to
the passionate lucidity of Fr. O'Mara's sermons? Would you
take my place, take me from my great vocation, and send me
off to be setting myself on fire in the great adventure of the
New World?

MICHAEL. There's still time.

PEGGY. What's he saying?

TOM. I've always taken my responsibilities seriously.

PEGGY. Of course you have, love.

TOM *is rolling his head in reaction to her.*

MICHAEL. What responsibilities for Christ's –

TOM. My mother, Jack, for Christ's sake, and my father, Jack, for Christ's sake. You enquired about my mother's health earlier but, for some strange reason or other, not my father's. Well, I can assure you they're both still alive – (*To* LIAM:) Don't be making wild-life faces at me, cowboy, I've got the goods on you!

LIAM. Didn't say a thing, fella.

Off, the town clock chiming ten.

MICHAEL. Do you know what he said about you one evening?

TOM. Who? (*Closes his eyes; he doesn't want to know.*) Oh yes, our president.

MICHAEL. That if you didn't break out of it, none of us would.

TOM (*continues with eyes shut*). Break out of what?

MICHAEL. This.

TOM. Are you speaking geographically?

MICHAEL. Not necessarily. This talk all evening, and what it seems to represent?

TOM. What does it represent?

MICHAEL. You'd think the sixties never happened.

TOM. What did the sixties represent?

MICHAEL. Not this.

TOM. You haven't answered-a-single-question-all-night. You, too, are a great dealer in the abstract.

MICHAEL. The social movements of the minority's groups in the sixties, in towns, villages and cities, was the rising culture.

TOM. And *is* this the *rising* culture, begod?

ANNE arrives with a tray of drinks.

ANNE. Scotch, Michael? –

TOM. Ah, God bless yeh, Anne! Because, despite the current swing to the right of the majorities, and the crusades of the christian fundamentalist majorities, promoting medieval notions of morality and reality, begod –

JUNIOR } Thanks, girl –

TOM } We the creative minorities are still here, begod, thank God, swinging to the left, while they're swinging to the right. But we, the swinging-to-the-lefters will see those swinging-to-the-righters go swinging to their decline and disintegration. For! – And! – As you say! – Even though we are the minority, it is always out of the creative cultural minority, it is always out of the creative cultural minority *groups* that change irrevocable comes about! – Begod! What do you think of that? (*To* MICHAEL.) Happy? He's not happy still –begod! And why would he? I left out the big one. (*He is searching his pockets for money for the round.*)

LIAM. Good luck, fellas!

TOM. Because – fellas! – despite us, the representatives of the rising cultural minorities aforementioned, what is going on now, this minute, ablow in Paddy Joe Daly's? 'Put th' fuckin' blanket on the ground.' (*They laugh.*) But Paddy Joe Daly is not the enemy. He may personify it, the bullets in his bandy legs may symbolise it, the antics of his lump of a wife may dramatise it. But no – No! – the real enemy – the big one! – that we shall overcome, is the country-and-western system itself. Unyielding, uncompromising, in its drive for total sentimentality. A sentimentality I say that would have us all an unholy herd of Sierra Sues, sad-eyed inquisitors, sentimental Nazis, fascists, sectarianists, black-and-blue shirted nationalists, with spurs a-jinglin', all ridin' down the trail to Oranmore. Aw great, I knew I'd make ye all happy.

They laugh.

JUNIOR. Aw, Jasus, the twins! (*He slips the money for the round to* ANNE.)

MICHAEL. Do you ever go for rambles down to Woodlawn like we used to, Anne?

ANNE. Sometimes.

And she moves off to answer a tapping on the counter in the public bar – a toss of her head and a smile back at MICHAEL.

JUNIOR. The two of ye together might make up one decent man.

TOM. Well, whatever about me, I don't know what reason you had to hang around here, Sonny.

JUNIOR. We've had the complimenting stage, let that be an end to the insulting stage, and we'll get on to the singing stage. (*Singing.*) 'All in the April evening' –

TOM. And your father won't leave you the garage. One of the young brothers will have that.

JUNIOR (*smile disappears*). They can have it so they can.

TOM. They will.

LIAM. And that's the belief in the town.

JUNIOR (*back in form*). No! No! They're all off, the whole seven of them, to join the Palestine Police Force next week. Wuw! Jasus, Jasus . . . ! Come on, Peggy, you're the singer here. 'All in the –

PEGGY. Oh stop, Junior.

JUNIOR. Come on, that one, JJ's song –

PEGGY. I don't know when I sang last.

JUNIOR. 'All in the April evening, April airs –'

PEGGY. Stop, Junie. No. No –

JUNIOR ⎱ 'The sheep with their little lambs –' Come on!
PEGGY ⎰ No, no, no, no, no –

JUNIOR ⎱ Come on, come on –
PEGGY ⎰ No, no, no, no, no –

LIAM (*about to sing*). Fellas!

PEGGY. Alright, so.

PEGGY *is standing up; she sings the first line of 'All in the April Evening'; then giggling, fixing herself into the pose of the amateur contralto at the wedding, and singing deliberately off key and 'poshly' distorting the words.*

'All in the April evening, April airs were abroad'. – No, wait a minute . . . 'This is my lovely dee. This is thee dee I shall remember the dee' – Christina Jordan, did you ever hear her? – 'I'll remember, I'll remember – !' The cheek of her, not a note right in her head – 'I'll remember, I'll remember –' Jeeney, the eejit! (*And she sits abruptly, hands over her mouth, giggling.*)

LIAM. Fellas!

TOM *exits to the Gents.*

(*Fancies himself as a cowboy singer.*) 'There's a bridle hanging on the wall/There's a saddle in a lonely stall/You ask me why my tear drops fall/It's that bridle hanging on the wall/And that pony for my guide I used to ride down the trail watching the moon beam low-ow – ' (*The others stifling their laughter at him.*)

MICHAEL *and* JUNIOR, *through the song.*

MICHAEL. I need a drop more water for this one.

JUNIOR. One voice! One voice!

MICHAEL *joins* ANNE *at the bar.*

LIAM. 'And the pony for my guide I used to ride down the trail/he's gone where the good ponies go-oh/There's a bridle hanging on the wall . . .' (*etc.*)

JUNIOR. Lovely hurlin', cowboy!

PEGGY. Smashin', Liam!

LIAM. I must mosey to the john again, fellas. Watch that latchyco, Anne! 'You ask me why my tear drops fall –'

TOM *entering as* LIAM *exits.*

TOM. And *your* sisters or young brother will have the farm.

LIAM. Sure, fella (*Exits, returns a moment later in response to* TOM's 'Hey!'.)

TOM. Hey! This eejit, this bollocks, with his auctioneering and tax-collecting and travel-agenting and property dealing and general greedy unprincipled poncing, and Sunday night dancing – Mr successful-swinging-Ireland-In-The-Seventies! – and he's still – Jesus! – watching the few acres of bog at home, still – Jesus! – caught up in the few acres of bog around the house at home.

LIAM. What – what would you say, fella, if I said it was mine already?

TOM. I'd say, fella, that you're a liar.

LIAM. Well, it is mine.

TOM. As the bishop said to the actress.

LIAM. By deed – by deed! – The deeds are signed over to me.

PEGGY. But why suddenly all this talk tonight?

LIAM. And my young brother is studying to be a doctor.

TOM. Weren't *you* studying to be a doctor?

LIAM. Oh, d'yeh hear him now?

TOM. And quietly, it was a fortuitous outcome for the sick and the ailing that you never made it.

LIAM. D'yeh hear him now – Tro'sky!

TOM. And even if the young brother proves less thick than you, haven't the two spinster sisters a claim on the place?

LIAM. By deed –

PEGGY. But why –

TOM. No – No deed! Because your attempts, and the details of your attempts, and the details of the failure of your attempts to unseat them and evict them off the nine-and-a-half acre O'Brady estate are widely discussed and reported upon – in this town.

LIAM. I'm setting up my sisters in an antique shop.

JUNIOR (*quietly*). That's the place for them.

TOM. And, quietly, and with little or no respect, I don't think either of them, in their advanced post-state of nubility, has much prospects of the bed.

LIAM. Oh d'yeh hear – I take exception to that remark!

TOM. Take what you like. Give us a drop of water here too for this one, Anne. So, the next time you see someone driving around in a Merc just think of him.

ANNE *arrives to add water to* TOM's *drink*.

LIAM. Why don't you get married?

TOM. Why don't yeh yourself? (*To* ANNE.) That's fine. (*He is rooting in his pockets again for further coins to pay for the last round.*)

LIAM. Afraid of his Mammy and Daddy. And, d'ye know, he has to hand over his paypacket to his Mammy, intact, every week, into her hand.

TOM. I get paid by cheque, Liam – monthly. (*To* ANNE.) Just a sec.

ANNE. It's paid for –

TOM. Just a sec –

LIAM. Then cheque, countersigned, it has to be handed over to Mammy.

PEGGY. Aa, change the subject, lads –

ANNE. Junie paid for it.

JUNIOR. Sure poor auld Liam could't go bringing a woman into a house where there's three of them already –

PEGGY (*offering* TOM *two pounds*). Here, love –

TOM (*to* ANNE). What?

JUNIOR. Jasus, they'd ate each other.

TOM (*to* LIAM). You are the worst of the worst type of a ponce of a modern fuckin' gombeen man, that's all that's to be said about it! (*to* ANNE). What?

ANNE. It's paid for, Tom.

LIAM. There's an answer for that one too.

TOM. Yes, Liam.

JUNIOR. It's paid for, it's okay –

LIAM (*only just containing his drunken fury*). My birthright!

TOM ⎱ (*to* JUNIOR). What? –
PEGGY ⎰ Here, loveen –
TOM ⎱ (*to* PEGGY). What? –
LIAM ⎰ That's no argument! –
TOM ⎱ (*to* LIAM). What?
JUNIOR ⎰ It's okay, it's paid for –

TOM. What?

LIAM. The eldest son, fella!

TOM (*to* LIAM). What are you talking about? (*To* ANNE.) And who asked anyone to pay for it! (*To himself.*) Tck! – Look – Jesus! – (*To* LIAM.) Look, don't talk to me about argument – Look – lookit, don't talk to me at all! (*To* PEGGY.) Will-you-put-that (*money*) – away! (*To* LIAM.) You're only a fuckin' bunch of keys! (*To* ANNE.) Bring us another round!

ANNE *returns to bar.*

PEGGY. Why don't you drive up and bring Gloria down. Do, Junie.

JUNIOR. Oh-oh.

PEGGY. Aa go on, good lad, do, do.

JUNIOR. Won't I be seeing her later!

LIAM. I'll squeeze your head for you some night, Ryan.

TOM. Good man. My round is coming, is it, Anne?

LIAM. Cause I hate ye all – and all belongin' to ye!

He sweeps up his newspaper, then wrong-foots himself in his indecision as to whether to leave or not, remembers he has a stake in the place and exits to the Gents.

JUNIOR. Once you go once you're knackered for the evening.

MICHAEL *laughing with* JUNIOR, *then* TOM *starts to chuckle and he joins* MICHAEL *and* ANNE *at the counter.*

ANNE. But he's a lovely dancer though.

TOM, MICHAEL, JUNIOR *laughing again.* ANNE *joining in.*

TOM. Now: the new generation: 'you ask me why my tear drops fall, it's that pony hangin' on the wall'.

Excepting PEGGY *they are laughing again. And* JUNIOR *is now rising to go to the Gents.*

JUNIOR. Jasus, Jasus – (*To* PEGGY.) Excuse me, the call of the wild, the enemy within – you have a great pair of kidneys, Ridge! Shake hands with the devil, wuw!

And he has exited to the Gents.

PEGGY *now continues self-consciously isolated at the table, her back to the others. And they have all but forgotten her.* TOM's *mood is now pacificatory.*

ANNE. What part are you in, Michael?

MICHAEL. Well, I'm not working, obviously at the moment, but –

TOM. What part of America she's asking, eejit.

MICHAEL *looks at him:* TOM *gestures/shrugs that no malice is intended.*

MICHAEL. New York.

ANNE. What's it like?

MICHAEL. Well, it's not too bad at all. Were you ever in the States?

ANNE. No, but I was in London last summer. Two of us went over and we stayed with some friends of daddy's.

MICHAEL. Did you? Did he arrange it for you?

ANNE. Yes.

PEGGY (*isolated*). Indeed I was there myself for a few months once.

Nobody is listening to her.

ANNE. We went to a place – I said I was eighteen – and got a job in an ice-cream factory.

PEGGY. I was putting the tops on polish tins.

ANNE *has set up the other round.*

TOM. Make that a double for your man (*Michael*) and mine the same and tell your mother to put it on the slate.

MICHAEL. I'll get it.

TOM. Don't be so extravagant with your mother's money. (*Then gestures/shrugs again to Michael's reaction; no malice intended; and showing Michael the few coins in his hand.*) Look at the way I am myself.

ANNE. And will I make the others doubles?

TOM. Are yeh coddin' me!

MICHAEL. What would you say to a stroll down to Woodlawn tomorrow, Anne?

She nods. This forthright reply, the immediate success of his proposition surprises and stops him for a moment.

ANNE. Fine.

MICHAEL. What?

ANNE. That'd be lovely . . . What time?

He gestures: what time would suit her?

Four?

MICHAEL (*nods*). . . . Where shall I . . . ? (*meet you*).

ANNE. The Bridge.

MICHAEL. Ah! The Bridge.

LIAM comes in and stands away from them, aloof, sulking. MICHAEL has started singing/performing – perhaps Rex Harrison/James Cagney style – for ANNE.

MICHAEL. 'At seventeen he falls in love quite madly with eyes of tender blue.'

TOM (*to LIAM*). There's a drink there for you, bollocks.

MICHAEL. 'At twenty-four, he gets it rather badly with eyes of different hue.'

TOM (*to ANNE*). Give him (*Liam*) that.

MICHAEL. 'At thirty-five, you'll find him flirting sadly with two, or three, or more.'

TOM (*edging him further away from the others*). Come over here a minute.

MICHAEL. 'When he fancies he is past love' –

TOM. This is nonsense, this caper all evening.

MICHAEL. 'It is then he meets his last love –'

TOM. Don't mind that. Hmm?

MICHAEL. Well, what's up with you?

TOM. Nothing. What's up with you?

MICHAEL. Not a thing.

TOM. Well then. Good luck!

MICHAEL. Good luck!

They toast each other. Short pause; they can't think of anything to say.

MICHAEL (*in* ANNE's *direction*). 'And he loves her as he's never loved before.'

TOM. I can't help it . . . I can't feel anything about anything anymore.

MICHAEL. I know.

TOM. What?

MICHAEL. I know what you mean.

TOM. You're the only friend I have . . . Wha'?

MICHAEL. Mutual.

TOM. Say something.

MICHAEL (*quietly*). Yahoo?

TOM. Did JJ admire me?

MICHAEL. Yeh.

TOM. But what good is that? I don't think he understood my — (*sighs*) — situation. Isn't that what people want? What? A true and honest account of the situation first. What? A bit of clarity and sanity. Definition. Facts. Wha'? . . . Did he admire me?

MICHAEL. Yeh.

TOM. More than the others, you said.

MICHAEL. Bigger expectations (*shrugs*) — I suppose.

TOM. What? . . . Will I tell you something: What? Will I? Will I tell you something confidential? What? Will I? I never lost an argument in my life. What? What d'yeh think of that? What? Isn't that something? . . . But you're doing well.

MICHAEL. No.

TOM. No! You are!

MICHAEL. Setting myself on fire.

TOM. You're doing well, you're doing well, someone has to be doing well, and we're all delighted, we are, we are, we really are . . . The only friend I have, bollocks, with your cigarette holder in your top pocket. (MICHAEL's *hand guiltily to his top pocket,* TOM, *intensely, drunkenly.*) Why didn't yeh use it, why didn't yeh use it?

MICHAEL. Just one of them filter things.

TOM. But why didn't yeh use it? D'yeh see what I mean? . . . (*Genuinely pained.*) I try. I can't help it.

PEGGY (*rising, approaching, smiling bravely*). What are the men talking about? I know well; the women are always left out of the juicy things.

TOM (*frowning to himself*). What?

PEGGY. Cheers!

TOM. What?

MICHAEL. Cheers, Peggy.

PEGGY. Do you ever meet anyone from round here over there, Michael?

MICHAEL. Oh, I met Casey.

PEGGY. Aa did yeh, Joe? D'yeh hear that, love? How's he getting on?

MICHAEL. Fine. Getting the dollars regular every week, hot and cold water in his room, and paying no income tax.

PEGGY. Indeed we heard the opposite –

TOM. Hold it a second, Peg –

PEGGY. Someone who saw him over there –

TOM. A minute, Peg –

PEGGY. No shirt, an old pullover, no heels to his shoes.

TOM. Why do you always reduce everything!

PEGGY. . . . Well it was you told me.

Off, the town clock ringing eleven.

MICHAEL. One for the road, Anne. (*Extricating himself from* TOM *and* PEGGY.)

JUNIOR (*off, and entering*). 'Oi, oi, oi, Delilah, phy, phy, phy, Delilah –' (*He surveys the room.*) Jasus, I was at better parties in the Mercy Convent!

MICHAEL (*kicking cigarette holder across the room*). I don't give a damn! A walk in the woods, a breath of fresh air! – Right Anne?

She laughs, nods.

JUNIOR. Into the net, Seaneen!

LIAM (*glowering; a warning*). Watch it! (*The cigarette holder flying past him.*)

JUNIOR. Keep the faith, cowboy! I'll sing a hymn to Mary, he says, the mother of them all! (*Sings.*) 'I'll sing a hymn' –

MICHAEL. No, nice and quiet, Junie. (*Sings.*) 'I'll sing a hymn to Mary . . .'

JUNIOR } 'The mother of my God . . .'
MICHAEL } 'The mother of my God, the virgin of all virgins –'

LIAM (ANNE *has brought a drink to him*). Nothing for me. (*He spills the drink* TOM *bought him and the one that has just arrived on the floor and continues brooding.*)

JUNIOR (*singing*). 'The virgin of all virgins of God's own dearly son!'

MICHAEL. 'Of David's royal blood'.

JUNIOR. 'Of David's royal blood'.

MICHAEL. Nice and quiet, Junie (*They sing together,* ANNE *singing with them:*) 'Oh teach me Holy Mary a loving song to frame/When wicked men blaspheme thee/I'll love and bless Thy name/Oh Lily of the Valley . . .' (*Etc., until it is stopped by* TOM's *attack on* PEGGY.)

TOM (*through the above, muttering*). Ugliness, ugliness, ugliness (*He becomes aware of* PEGGY.) What are you looking at?

PEGGY *has been casting hopeful glances at him. She does not reply,* MICHAEL, JUNIOR *and* ANNE *continue softly – under the following:*

TOM (*to* PEGGY). Do even *you* admire me? My feverish social writings.

PEGGY. It's late, love.

TOM. My generous warm humour.

PEGGY. I'd like to go home, love.

TOM. What?

PEGGY. I don't feel well, love.

TOM. Well, go! Who's stopping yeh? My God, you walk up and down from your own house twenty times a day with your short little legs! No one will molest you! We're all mice!

She hurries from the room, stops in the front doorway, can't leave, her life invested in TOM *— and hangs in the doorway crying. Off, the church clock ringing eleven.*

MICHAEL (*about to follow* PEGGY). Ah Jesus, sham.

TOM (*stops him with his voice*). Hey! (*Then:*) Ugliness, ugliness, ugliness!

ANNE. She's not feeling well.

TOM (*stopping* MICHAEL *again with his voice and warning him not to interfere*). Hey! Gentlemen! Jim! My extravagant adventurous spirit. And the warm wild humour of Liam over there. And all those men of prudence and endeavour who would sell the little we have left of charm, character, kindness and madness to any old bidder with a pound, a dollar, a mark or a yen. And all those honest and honourable men who campaign for the right party and collect taxes on the chapel road. And all those honest and honourable men who are cutting down the trees for making — Easter-egg boxes!

MICHAEL. That's more like it!

TOM. Is it? (*Stopping* MICHAEL *again from going out to* PEGGY.) Hey!

JUNIOR (*quietly to* MICHAEL). Leave it so.

MICHAEL. Let us remember that civility is not a sign of weakness —

TOM (*mimics Kennedy*). 'And that sincerity is always subject to proof.' You all love speeches, rhetoric, crap, speeches. Right! 'I know you all, and will a while uphold the unyoked humour of your idleness.' I was always a better actor than you, better at everything than anyone round here. 'Yet herein will I imitate the sun who doth permit the base contagious clouds to smother up his beauty from the world!'

MICHAEL. 'But when he please again to be himself —'

TOM. *That!* 'That when he please again to be himself, being
wanted, he may be more wondered at, by breaking through
the foul and ugly mists of vapour that seem to strangle him,'
tangle him, bangle him . . .

VOICE (*off*). Goodnight to ye now.
JUNIOR Good luck, Johnny!
ANNE Good night, Johnny!
MICHAEL Deoch an dorais, Tom, come on.

TOM (*quietly: going – now docilely – to bar with* MICHAEL).
'And when this loose behaviour I throw off, by how much
better than my word I am, my reformation glittering o'er my
faults shall show more goodly and attract more eyes than this
which hath no foil to set it off.'

Through this last section, PEGGY *is in the doorway – she has
had her head to the wall, crying – now listening, hoping
someone will come out to her. She starts to sing – at first
tentatively, like someone making noises to attract attention to
herself. Then progressively, going into herself, singing
essentially for herself; quietly, looking out at the night, her
back to us, the sound representing her loneliness, the gentle
desperation of her situation, and the memory of a decade ago.
Her song creates a stillness over them all.*

PEGGY. 'All in the April evening, April airs were abroad/ The
sheep with their little lambs passed me by on the road/ The
sheep with their little lambs passed me by on the road/ All in
the April evening I thought on the lamb of God.'

At the conclusion of the song, MISSUS *coming down the
stairs.* PEGGY *instinctively moving out of the doorway to
stand outside the pub.*

TOM (*quietly*). 'I'll so offend to make offence a skill, redeeming
time when men think least I will.'

MISSUS *comes in to collect a broom.*

MISSUS. Come on now, boys, it's gone the time.

TOM. One for the road, Missus.

MISSUS (*returning to the public bar*). And Johnny Quinn is half-way home the back way to his bed by now.

JUNIOR. Well, that's it.

LIAM. Well, that's not it! (*He rattles a chair: his statement of challenge to fight.*) I can quote more Shakespeare than any man here! (*He glances at each of them in turn, culminating with TOM.*)

MISSUS (*off*). Drink up now boys!

LIAM. 'And still they marvelled and the wonder grew, that one *big* head could carry all he knew.'

TOM (*eyes closed*). Shakespeare?

LIAM. No. Goldsmith.

JUNIOR. Well said, boy.

LIAM. *The Deserted Village*, fella.

MISSUS (*off*). Finish up now, boys!

LIAM. Ryan! The village schoolmaster . . .The f-f-f- . . . The f-f-f- . . . Ryan!

LIAM *breathing heavily through his nose, jaws set, fists clenched*. TOM, *still with eyes closed, arms limply at his sides, turns to LIAM, nods, prepared to be hit, perhaps wanting to be hit.*

The village schoolmaster.

TOM *eyes closed, nods again. LIAM unsure as to whether or not he is being mocked, glancing at the others . . . then suddenly grabs TOM's hand and shakes it.*

MISSUS (*coming in with broom which she gives to ANNE*). And the guards are on the prowl these nights.

TOM (*to LIAM*). So, are we quits?

LIAM. Okay, fella.

TOM (*glancing at MICHAEL*). But we're not quite through.

PEGGY *comes in timidly, gets her coat, hopeful glances at* TOM.

They all speak at once:

MICHAEL. We're going to start again with a constant flow of good ideas. 'Let the word go forth . . .'

TOM (*by way of apology to* PEGGY). Just . . . a bit of Shakespeare.

MICHAEL. 'From this time and place, to friend and foe alike, that the torch has been passed to a new generation.'

MISSUS. Come on now, boys, come on.

JUNIOR. Well I must be getting home anyway to Gloria – Oosh!

MICHAEL. 'Let every nation know, whether it wishes us good or ill, that we shall pay any price, bear any burden, endure any hardship, to ensure the success and the survival of liberty.'

MISSUS (*to* LIAM). Call again during the week, Liam – why wouldn't yeh – and have a nice bite of tea with us. And thanks, the good boy, Liam. Drink up now, boys, and haven't ye all night tomorrow night, and thanks, thank ye all now. Yas. And safe home. D'ye know now.

She has switched off the lights in the lounge – (the spill of light from the hallway and from the public bar now light the lounge) – and she is on her way along the hallway, upstairs, counting the money from her cardigan pockets. ANNE *is about to exit with the broom and some dirty glasses to public bar.*

MICHAEL. Goodnight, princess, till it be morrow!

ANNE. Goodnight. (*And exits to public bar.*)

They are pulling on their coats, etc. in silence. JUNIOR *scrutinising the table for any drink that might have been left unfinished.*

MICHAEL. But it wasn't a bad night.

JUNIOR. It wasn't a bad auld night alright. (*And eager for further confirmation of this.*) Wha'?

LIAM (*muttering*). I wouldn't advise anyone to go messing with my plans.

MICHAEL. And I'll be wheeling Annette tomorrow.

TOM. Good man.

LIAM (*muttering*). I know a thing or two about you, Ridge.

PEGGY. What's he muttering about?

MICHAEL (*singing quietly*). 'Sure no letter I'll be mailin' ' –

LIAM. It's not right.

MICHAEL. 'For soon will I be sailin' ' –

PEGGY. Brrah! Come on, loveen, I'm perished.

TOM (*sudden thought*). Wait a minute.

MICHAEL. 'And I'll bless the ship that takes me –'

TOM. It's not right alright –

MICHAEL. 'To my dear auld Erin's shore –'

TOM. Michael. Anne.

MICHAEL｜ 'There I'll settle down forever –'
TOM　　 ⎬ Serious – Michael – Don't start messin'.
MICHAEL｜ What?

LIAM. Don't start messin' fella. Invested time and money. My – our territory. Right, Tom? Junie?

MICHAEL (*laughs*). 'There's a pretty spot in Ireland —'

TOM. Michael. Are you listening?

MICHAEL. It's not a jiggy-jig job. JJ's daughter. A walk in the wood, a breath of fresh air. (*He looks at their serious faces.*) You know it's nothing else.

TOM. We don't.

LIAM. We don't, fella. A word to Mrs Kilkelly – or to Anne herself.

TOM. So cop on.

MICHAEL. Who?

TOM. You.

LIAM. You, fella. Don't infringe.

MICHAEL *looks incredulously at* TOM.

TOM (*shrugs/blandly*). Liam's territory. Right Liam, you nearly have it sold, right? Good. Even if they don't know it. Better for Missus, Anne, better for – Put a bomb under it if you like – better for everyone. Reality. So that's okay. And we'll fix you up with the gammy one tomorrow. Josphine. Right, Junie?

JUNIOR (*has enough of them*). I'm off. Jasus, I only meant to have the two pints. (*To* MICHAEL.) D'yeh want a lift? (*To* TOM *and* PEGGY.) D'ye want a life? Okay, see ye.

He goes off, puffing a tuneless whistle and a few moments later we hear him drive away.

PEGGY. Oh come on, loveen, your mother will have your life.

TOM. Don't be silly!

LIAM. So that's okay then, Tom?

TOM (*quietly but firmly*). Yeh.

LIAM. Okay, fellas, God bless.

He exits.

TOM. . . . . I hope he remembers he has no clutch in his car or he'll be all night looking for it.

LIAM's *car starting up and driving away.*

Come on, we'll walk you home.

MICHAEL. I'm dead sober. And I'm certainly not as confused as I was.

TOM (*pacificatory*). Ary! You're only an eejit, Ridge.

MICHAEL *nods.*

PEGGY. Y'are.

MICHAEL *nods.*

TOM (*mock gruffness*). Y'are!

MICHAEL. But I know what I came home for.

TOM. Come on, we'll walk yeh down.

MICHAEL. No. I'm okay.

TOM. Give us a shout tomorrow.

PEGGY. Night-night, Michael.

TOM. We didn't get a chance to have a right talk.

PEGGY. God bless, take care.

TOM. Good luck, sham.

MICHAEL. Good luck.

TOM *and* PEGGY *have left.*

TOM (*off*). Give us a shout tomorrow!

PEGGY (*off*). 'Bye-'bye, Michael!

TOM (*off*). Will yeh?

PEGGY (*off*). 'Bye-'bye, Michael!

TOM (*off*). Will yeh?

PEGGY (*off*). 'Bye-'bye!

MICHAEL *continues standing there. He looks up and around at the room. He finishes his drink and is about to leave.*

MISSUS (*off*). Leave the light on in the hall, Annette, in case.

The light is switched off in the public bar and ANNE enters and discovers MICHAEL. Her simple grave expression.

MICHAEL (*whispers*). I have to go in the morning.

ANNE (*silently*). What?

MICHAEL. Have to go in the morning. (*He smiles, shrugs.*) They've probably cut down the rest of the wood by now, anyway.

ANNE. There's still the stream.

MICHAEL. Yeh. But I have to go. Tell JJ I'm sorry I didn't see him. Tell him . . . (*He wants to add something but cannot find the words yet.*) . . . Tell him I love him.

She nods, she smiles, she knows. He waits for another moment to admire her, then he walks off. ANNE continues in the window as at the beginning of the play, smiling her gentle hope out at the night.

Bailegangaire

The Story of Bailegangaire
and how it came by its appellation

Bailegangaire was first performed by the Druid Theatre Company, Galway, on 5 December 1985 with the following cast:

MOMMO	Siobhán McKenna
MARY	Marie Mullen
DOLLY	Mary McEvoy

Directed by Garry Hynes
Designed by Frank Conroy
Lighting by Roger Frith

Time and place: 1984, the kitchen of a thatched house. The set should be stylized to avoid cliché and to achieve best effect.

Note: 'Notturno' in E Flat by Schubert introduces and closes the play. Mary's poem, which she misquotes, in Act One is 'Silences' by Thomas Hardy.

ACT ONE

Dusk is setting in. The room is a country kitchen in the old style. There are some modern conveniences: a bottle-gas cooker, a radio, electric light – a single pendant. Framed photographs on the walls, brown photographs of uncles, one of a christening party. There is a double bed in the kitchen – it is the warmest room in the house (probably the central room of the traditional three-roomed thatched house). An old woman in the bed, MOMMO, is eating and drinking something out of a mug, occasionally rejecting pieces of food, spitting them on the floor. She is a good mimic. She interrupts her meal –

MOMMO. Scoth caoc! Shkoth!

Driving imagined hens from the house.

Dirty aul' things about the place . . . And for all they lay!

She is senile.

MARY, *her granddaughter, is seated beside the fire, looking at nothing, not even at the fire. She wears a wrap-around apron draped tightly about her spinster frame; bare knees over half wellington boots; hair tight, perhaps in a bun. She is forty-one. A 'private' person, an intelligent, sensitive woman, a trier, but one who is possibly near breaking point. It is lovely when she laughs. She does not react to the above. MOMMO has again interrupted her meal this time to talk to imagined children at the foot of the bed.*

Let ye be settling now, my fondlings, and I'll be giving ye a nice story tonight when I finish this. For isn't it a good one? An' ye'll be goin' to sleep.

The tips of MARY's *fingers to her forehead and she closes her eyes.*

. . . Oh ho, but he bet (*beat*) them. He bet the best of them . . . Incestuous drunkards and bastards.

The kettle on the gas stove is whistling. MARY *rises mechanically to make tea, lay the table. She produces the anomaly of a silver teapot . . .* MOMMO *is now watching* MARY *and* MARY's *movements suspiciously.*

. . . An' no one will stop me! Tellin' my nice story . . . (*Reverts to herself.*) Yis, how the place called Bochtán – and its *graund* (*grand*) inhabitants – came by its new appellation, Bailegangaire, the place without laughter. Now! .   Jolter-headed gobshites . . . (*Grandly.*) Ooh! and to be sure, and I often heard it said, it had one time its portion of jollification and mirth. But, I'm thinkin', the breed they wor (*were*) 'twas venom, and the dent of it, was ever the more customary manifestation. The land there so poor – Och hona go gus hah-haa, land! – when 'twasn't bog 'twas stone, and as for the weather? 'twas credited with bein' seven times worse than elsewhere in the kingdom. And so hard they had it, to keep life itself in them, whenever Bochtán was mentioned the old people in their wisdom would add in precaution, go bhfóire Dia orainn, may God protect us. What time is it?

MARY. Seven.

MARY *is taking off her apron.*

MOMMO. Yis! Shkoth! – an' lock them in. Och haw, but I'll out-do the fox. I'll take the head of the everyone of them tomorrow. Ooh! and to be sure –

MARY (*quietly*). Mommo?

MOMMO. And I often heard it said –

MARY. Mommo? (*She has removed her apron and in her new image is smiling bravely against an increasing sense of loneliness and demoralisation.*) I have a surprise for you.

MOMMO. Pardon?

MARY. Look! (*She holds up an iced cake.*) We never knew your birthday but today is mine and I thought we might share the same birthday together in future. (*She has lit a candle.*)

MOMMO (*eyes fixed on the candle*). The cursèd paraffin.

MARY. Though someone said once – I may be wrong – yours was the first of May, a May child – But look! –

MOMMO. The cursèd paraffin.

MARY. And the candles. And another (*candle*) here, and you can get out of bed for a little – if you wish.

MOMMO. Birthday?

MARY. Yes! We'll have a party, the two of us.

MOMMO. What's birthdays to do with us?

MARY. By candlelight.

MOMMO. What's your business here?

MARY (*indicating the table*). Isn't that nice?

MOMMO. Do I know you?

MARY. Mary. (*She bows her head, momentarily deflated, then smiles invitingly at MOMMO again.*)

MOMMO (*and there is defiance, hatred in the sound*). Heh heh heh heh.

MARY. Mary.

MARY *picks up a book en route to switch on the radio and sits at the table to have her tea. We get the end of the news in Irish on the radio, then Tommy O'Brien's programme of light classics,* Your Choice and Mine. *The candlelight, the table neatly laid, the silver teapot, the simple line of Mary's dress becomes her, the book beside her, sipping tea, the grave intelligent face, a picture of strange elegance.* MOMMO *has been continuing.*

MOMMO. Ooh! and to be sure and so as not to be putting any over-enlargement on my narrative, the creatures left in it now can still *smile*, on occasion. And to be sure, the childre, as is the wont of all childre in God's kingdom on earth, are as clever at the laughing as they are at the crying, until they arrive at the age of reason. That is well, my dears. Now to tell my story. Here! You! Miss! Take this. Did you manage to poison me! Ha-haa – No – ho-ho!

MARY (*takes a cup of tea to* MOMMO *and places it on the chair beside the bed, takes the mug*). And I'll get you a nice slice of cake to go with the tea.

MOMMO. Pardon?

MARY. And isn't that nice music?

MOMMO. Cake?

MARY. Every Sunday night.

MOMMO. Music?

MARY. Yes. Listen.

MOMMO. . . . An' no one will stop me tellin' it!

MARY, *suspended in the action of about to cut the cake, now sits at the table, lights a cigarette, face impassive, exhaling smoke.*

MOMMO (*settles herself in the bed for her story*). Now . . . It was a bad year for the crops, a good one for mushrooms and the contrary and adverse connection between these two is always the case. So you can be sure the people were putting their store in the poultry and the bonavs (*bonhams*) and the creamery produce for the great maragadh mór (*big market*) that is held every year on the last Saturday before Christmas in Bailethuama (the town of Tuam) in the other county. And some sold well and some sold middlin', and one couple was in it – strangers, ye understand – sold not at all. And at day's business concluded there was celebration, for some, and fitting felicitations exchanged, though not of the usual protraction, for all had an eye on the cold inclement weather that boded. So, the people were departing Bailethuama in the other county in diverse directions homewards. As were the people of the place I'm talking about. And they were only middlin' satisfied, if at all. The Bochtáns were never entirely fortunate. An' devil mend them. An' scald them. No matter. What time is it? . . Miss!

MARY. Seven. Eight. (*The tips of her fingers to her forehead.*)

MOMMO. I'm waiting for someone. Supa tea.

MARY. It's on the chair beside you.

MOMMO. Oh an' he *will* come yet. (*A warning to MARY.*) And he has a big stick.

MARY (*remains seated: she knows from experience what the outcome of the conversation is going to be; she does not lift her eyes*). And time to take your pills.

MOMMO (*has no intention of taking them*). The yellow ones?

MARY. Yes.

MOMMO. They're good for me?

MARY. I'll give you a cigarette.

MOMMO. They'll help me sleep?

MARY. Yes.

MOMMO. Heh heh heh heh.

MARY (*to herself*). And I'd like to read, Mommo.

MOMMO. Now there was a decent man at that market and his decent wife the same. Strangers, strangers! Sure they could have come from the south of – Galway! – for all I know. And they had sold not at all. Well, if you call the one basket of pullets' eggs valiant trade. (*She takes a sip of the tea.*) Too hot. No.Their main cargo which consisted of eighteen snow-white geese still lay trussed in the floor of the cart, 'gus bhár ar an mi-ádh sin (*and to make matters worse*) the pitch on an incline of the road was proving an impossibility for the horse to surmount. But he was a decent man, and he took not belt – nor the buckle-end of it as another would – to the noble animal that is the horse. Put it down. (*The last to MARY who is standing by having put a little more milk into MOMMO's tea.*) No. But spoke only in the gentlest of terms, encouraging the poor beast to try once more against the adversary. 'Try again, Pedlar.' For that was the horse's name. Is that a step?

MARY (*listening*). . . . Dolly was to call last night. (*The sound they have heard – if any – does not materialise further.*) Nobody. She didn't call the night before either.

MOMMO. What's this?

MARY *does not understand.*

Taking down the good cup!

MARY. It tastes nicer out of a –

MOMMO. Mug, a mug! – oh leave it so now! Put it down!

MARY. And nicer to have your pills with.

MOMMO. The yellow ones? – Try again, Pedlar, for-that-was-the-horse's name!

MARY *returns to the table.*

And all the while his decent wife on the grass verge and she cráite (*crestfallen*). And a detail which you may contemplate fondly now but was only further testimonial to the misfortunes of that unhappy couple, each time she went to draw the shawl more tightly round her frailty, the hand peepin' out held three sticks of rock. Now! Yis, gifts for her care, three small waiting grandchildren. Like ye. Isn't it a good one? (*A sip of tea.*) Cold.

MARY (*to herself*). I can't stand it.

But she is up again in a moment to add a little hot water and a little more sugar to the tea.

MOMMO. And she up to the fifty mark!

MARY (*to herself*). And that bitch Dolly.

MOMMO. Or was she maybe more?

MARY. In heat again.

MOMMO. And what was her husband? Decorous efficiency in all he cared to turn his hand to, like all small men. Sure he had topped the sixty!

MARY. Taste that and see if it's alright for you.

MOMMO. But he was unlucky. He was. He was. An' times, maybe, she was unkind to him. (*Childlike.*) Was she?

MARY. No. (*Returning to the table where she sits, her head back on her shoulders, looking up at the ceiling.*)

MOMMO. And how many children had she bore herself?

MARY. Eight?

MOMMO. And what happened to them?

MARY. Nine? Ten?

MOMMO. Hah?

MARY. What happened us all?

MOMMO. Them (*that*) weren't drowned or died they said she drove away.

MARY. Mommo?

MOMMO. Let them say what they like.

MARY. I'm very happy here.

MOMMO. Hmmph!

MARY. I'm Mary.

MOMMO. Oh but she looked after her grandchildren.

MARY. Mommo?

MOMMO. And Tom is in Galway. He's afeared of the gander.

MARY. But I'm so . . . (*She leaves it unfinished, she can't find the word.*)

MOMMO. To continue.

MARY. Please stop. (*She rises slowly.*)

MOMMO. Now man and horse, though God knows they tried, could see the icy hill was not for yielding.

MARY. Because I'm so lonely.

She puts on her apron mechanically, then sets to work. Progressively working harder: scrubbing that part of the floor MOMMO *has spat upon, clearing away and washing up the crockery, washing clothes that have been soaking in a bucket . . . Later in the play, working, working: sheets to be put soaking in a bucket overnight, a bucket of mash for the hends in the morning, bringing in the turf . . .*

MOMMO. So what was there for doing but to retrace the hard-won steps to the butt-end of the road which, as matters would have it, was a fork. One road leading up the incline whence they came, the other to Bochtán.

Now that man knew that the road to Bochtán, though of circularity, was another means home. And it looked level enough stretching out into the gathering duskess. And 'deed he knew men from his own village (*who*) had travelled it and

got home safe and sound. Still he paused. Oh not through
fear, for if he was a man to submit he would've threwn
himself into the river years ago. No. But in gentleness, sad the
searching eye on the road. And sadder still the same grey eyes
were growing in handsomeness as the years went by. She had
noted it. But she'd never comment on this becoming aspect of
his mien for, strange, it saddened her too. It did. But the two
little smiles appearing, one each side of his mouth, before
taking a step anywhere. Even when only to go to the back
door last thing at night an' call in the old dog to the hearth.

MARY *hears the 'putt-putt' of a motorcycle approaching,*
stopping outside. She pauses in her work for a moment.
Then:

MARY. Right!

Suggesting she is going to have matters out with DOLLY.
DOLLY *comes in. Like her name, dolled-up, gaudy rural*
fashion. She is perhaps carrying a crash-helmet. She is thirty-
nine. MOMMO *is paused in her own thoughts and does not*
notice DOLLY's *entrance;* MARY *does not acknowledge it,*
she has resumed working. DOLLY *remains with her back to*
the front door for some time.

MOMMO. . . . Last thing at night . . . An' then the silence,
save the tick of the clock . . . An' why didn't she break it? She
knew how to use the weapon of silence. But why didn't he? A
woman isn't stick or stone. The gap in the bed, concern for
the morrow, how to keep the one foot in front of the other.
An' when would it all stop .   What was the dog's name?
(*Childlike.*) D'ye know I can't remember.

DOLLY. Mo Dhuine (*The One*).

MOMMO. Shep, was it?

DOLLY. Mo Dhuine.

MOMMO. Spot? Rover? . . . Mo Dhuine! Mo Dhuine! Now!
Mo Dhuine.

DOLLY. Jesus.

MOMMO. He loved Mo Dhuine – Och hona ho gus ha-haa! – An' the bother an' the care on him one time filling the eggshell with the hot ember an' leavin' it there by the door.

DOLLY. Then the root in the arse.

MOMMO. Then the root in the arse to poor Mo Dhuine, the twig 'cross his back, to get along with him an' the mouth burned in him! Oh but it did, *did*, cured him of thievin' the eggs.

DOLLY *switches on the light.*
MOMMO'*s eyes to the light bulb.*

DOLLY. What're yeh doin' workin' in the dark?

MOMMO. But they had to get home.

DOLLY. Oh, she can't have everything her own way.

MOMMO. Their inheritance, the three small waiting children, left unattended.

DOLLY (*rooting in her bag, producing a bottle of vodka*). How yeh!

MARY *merely nods, continues working.*

MOMMO. And night fast closing around them.

DOLLY. Stronger she's gettin'. A present.

MARY (*hopeful that the vodka is for her birthday*). For what?

DOLLY. 'Cause I couldn't come up last night.

MARY. What do I! (*want with a bottle of vodka*)

DOLLY. Yeh never know. She'll last forever.

MOMMO. Then, drawing a deep breath. (*She draws a deep breath.*) Oh but didn't give vent to it, for like the man he was I'm sayin', refusing to *sigh* or submit. An', 'On we go, Pedlar' says he, an' man, horse, cart, and the woman falling in between the two hind shafts set off on the road to Bochtán which place did not come by its present appellation, Bailegangaire, till that very night. Now.

DOLLY. Jesus, Bailegangaire – D'yeh want a fag? – night after night, can't you stop her. A fag?

MARY (*declines the cigarette*). No.

DOLLY. Night after night the same old story – (*Proffering cigarettes again.*) Ary you might as well.

MARY *ignores her.*

By Jesus I'd stop her.

MARY. I wish you'd stop using that word, Dolly. I've been trying to stop her.

DOLLY. Michaeleen is sick. The tonsils again. So I couldn't come up last night. I'm worried about them tonsils. What d'yeh think? So I can't stay long tonight either.

MARY *sighs.*

MOMMO. But to come to Bailegangaire so ye'll have it all.

MARY. Aren't you going to say hello to her?

DOLLY. What's up with yeh?

MARY. Nothing.

MOMMO. Them from that place had been to the market were 'riving back home.

DOLLY. *Home*, I'm goin'.

MOMMO. One of them, Séamus Costello by name.

MARY. Aren't you going to take off your coat?

DOLLY. What do you mean?

MOMMO. Oh a fine strappin' man.

MARY. What do you mean what do I mean!

DOLLY *turns stubbornly into the fire.*

MOMMO. Wherever he got it from. The size an' the breadth of him, you'd near have to step into the verge to give him sufficient right-of-way. 'Twould be no use him extending the

civility 'cause you'd hardly get around him I'm saying. And
he was liked. Rabbits he was interested in. This to his
widowed mother's dismay, but that's another thing. And the
kind of man that when people'd espy him approaching the
gurgle'd be already startin' in their mouths – Och-haw. For
he was the exception, ye understand, with humour in him as
big as himself. And I'm thinkin' he was the one an' only boast
they ever had in that cursèd place. What time is it?

MARY ⎱ Eight.
DOLLY ⎰ Nine.

They look at each other and bygones are bygones.

MARY. Quarter past eight.

MOMMO. Quarter past eight, an' sure that's not late. That's a
rhyme. Now for ye! (*She takes a sip of tea.*) Too sweet.

*MARY rectifying the tea situation. A cajoling tone coming
into DOLLY's voice – there is something on her mind, and
she is watching and assessing MARY privately.*

DOLLY. They say it's easier to do it for someone else's (*to take
care of a stranger*). (*Declining tea which MARY offers.*) No
thanks. And that old story is only upsetting her, Mary. Isn't
it?

*MARY is too intelligent to be taken in by DOLLY's tone or
tactics – but this is not at issue here: she has other things on
her mind. She sits by the fire with DOLLY and now accepts
the cigarette. MOMMO is sipping tea.*

Harping on misery. And only wearing herself out. And you.
Amn't I right, Mary? And she never finishes it – Why doesn't
she finish it? And have done with it. For God's sake.

*MARY considers this ('Finish it? And have done with it.'),
then forgets it for the moment. She is just looking into the
fire.*

MARY. I want to have a talk to you, Dolly.

DOLLY (*cautiously*). . . . About what?

MARY. Do you remember . . . (*She shakes her head: she does not know.*)

DOLLY. . . . What? . . . I know it affects you. Like, her not reco'nisin' you ever — Why wouldn't it? But you were away a long time.

MARY *looks up: she has been only half listening.*

That's the reason.

MARY. . . . I've often thought . . . (*Just looking at the fire again.*)

DOLLY. . . . What?

MARY. I may have been too — bossy, at first.

DOLLY. Well, well, there could be something in that, too.

MARY. But I wanted to . . . bring about change. Comfort, civilized.

DOLLY. Yes, well, but. Though I don't know. You were away an awful long time. I was left holdin' the can. Like, when yeh think of it, you owe me a very big debt.

MARY (*looks up*). Hmm: A very big?

DOLLY. I mean that's why she reco'nises me.

MARY *looking at the fire again;* DOLLY *watching MARY. Something on DOLLY's mind; she coughs in preparation to speak —*

MARY. We had a pony and trap once. The Sunday outings. You don't remember?

DOLLY, *puzzled, shakes her head.*

Ribbons. Grandad would always bring ribbons home for our hair. You don't remember.

DOLLY. . . . You work too hard.

MARY *laughs to herself at the remark.*

DOLLY (*laughs*). What?

MARY *shakes her head.*

DOLLY. And you're too serious.

MARY. Do you remember Daddy?

DOLLY. Well, the photographs.

They glance at the framed photographs on the wall.

Aul' brown ghosts. (*Playful, but cajoling.*) Y'are, y'are, too serious.

MARY (*eyes back to the fire*). I suppose I am. I don't know what I'm trying to say. (*Sighs.*) Home.

MOMMO (*has put down her cup*). And that, too, is well.

DOLLY. What?

MARY, *another slight shake of her head: she doesn't know.*

MOMMO. And now with his old jiggler of a bicycle set again' the gable, Costello was goin' in to John Mah'ny's, the one and only shop for everything for miles around.

DOLLY (*to MARY*). What?

MOMMO. 'Cold enough for ye, ladies!' Now! Cold enough for ye, ladies. And that was the first remark he was to utter that evening. And the two women he had thus accosted set to gurgling at once and together. 'Caw och-caw. Seamusheen a wockeen, God bless yeh, och-caw,' says the old crone that was in it buyin' the salt. And, 'Uck-uck-uck, uck-uck hunuka huckina-caw, Costello' from the young buxom woman tendin' the shop end of the counter, and she turnin' one of the babes in her arms so that he too could behold the hero. 'Aren't they gettin' awful big, God bless them,' then saying Costello of the two twins an' they gogglin' at him. 'Jack Frost is coming with a vengeance for ye tonight,' says he, 'or the Bogey Man maybe bejingoes'. And to the four or five others now holding tight their mother's apron, 'Well, someone is

comin' anyways,' says he, 'if ye all aren't good'. An' then off
with him to the end where the drink was.

DOLLY. Good man Josie!

MARY. No!

MOMMO } 'Good man, Josie!'
MARY   } Don't encourage her.

MOMMO } Now!
MARY   } I'm –! (going out of my mind).

MOMMO } Good man, Josie.
MARY   } I'm trying to stop it!

MOMMO } And that was the second greeting he uttered that
       }   night.
MARY   } Talk to her!
DOLLY } That's what I try to do!

MOMMO. He got no reply.

DOLLY (going to MOMMO, under her breath). Good man
  Josie, Jesus!

MOMMO. Nor did he expect one.

DOLLY (calling back to MARY). And I'm going at quarter to
  nine! – Good man, Mommo, how's it cuttin'?

MOMMO. Good man – ! Pardon?

DOLLY. How's the adversary treatin' yeh?

MOMMO (to herself). Good man Mommo?

DOLLY. I brought yeh sweets.

MOMMO. There's nothing wrong with me.

DOLLY. I didn't say there was.

MOMMO. An' I never done nothin' wrong.

DOLLY. Sweets!

MARY. Butterscotch, isn't it, Dolly?

MOMMO (to herself, puzzled again). Good man – Who?

DOLLY. Butterscotch, I've oceans of money.

MARY. Your favourites.

DOLLY. You like them ones.

MARY. Try one. You (DOLLY) give it to her.

MOMMO. Do I like them ones?

MARY. Suck it slowly.

DOLLY. Gob-stoppers I should have brought her.

MARY. Shh!

DOLLY. You're lookin' fantastic, (*Going back to the fire.*) It'd be a blessing if she went.

MARY (*placatory*). Shh, don't say things like (*that*). Talk to her, come on.

DOLLY. About what? It's like an oven in here – and I don't understand a word she's sayin'.

MARY. Take off your – (*coat*).

DOLLY. I – don't – want – to – take – off – my! –

MARY. Tell her about the children.

DOLLY. Seafóid, nonsense talk about forty years ago –

MARY. Come on –

DOLLY. And I've enough problems of my own. Why don't you stick her in there? (*One of the other rooms.*)

MARY. It's damp. And she understands – recognises you a lot of the time.

DOLLY *rolling her eyes but following* MARY *back to the bed again.*

Where she can see you.

DOLLY. Well, the children are all fine, Mommo. (*A slip*). Well, Michaeleen is sick, the tonsils again. I've rubber-backed lino in all the bedrooms now, the Honda is going like a bomb and the *lounge*, my dear, is carpeted. I seen the lean and lanky May Glynn, who never comes near ye or this house, in the garden when I was motoring over but she went in without a salute. I must have distemper too, or whatever. Conor, that other lean and lanky bastard, is now snaking his fence in another six inches, and my darlin' mother-in-law, old sharp-eyes-and-the-family rosary, sends her pers'nal blessings to ye both. Now. Darlin's.

MARY. Is she babysittin' for you?

DOLLY. No. She is not babysitting for me. I don't want her or any of the McGrath clan in my house. But I have someone babysittin' – since you're lookin' concerned.

MARY. I wasn't.

MOMMO (*sucking the sweet*). They're nice.

DOLLY. An' the cat had kittens. (*To* MARY.) D'yeh want a kitten? Do you, Mommo? (*A touch of sour, introversion.*) Does anyone? Before I drown them.

MOMMO. Tom is in Galway.

MARY. Did you hear from Stephen?

DOLLY. The 'wire' again on Friday, regular as clockwork.

MARY. Did you hear, Mommo?

MOMMO. I did. But she told May Glynn not to be waitin', her own mother'd be needin' her, and that they'd be home before dark for sure.

DOLLY. Eighty-five quid a week and never a line.

MARY. He's busy.

DOLLY (*to herself*). Fuck him. I don't know what to do with the money! (*Sudden introspection again.*) Or do I? I've started saving. (*Then impetuously:*) Do *you* want some? Well, do you, Mommo? To go dancin'.

MARY *is laughing at her sister's personality.*

What?

MARY. Stephen will be home as usual for Christmas.

DOLLY. For his goose.

MARY. Won't he, Mommo?

MOMMO (*to herself*). Stephen, yes, fugum.

They laugh. Then, Dolly grimly:

DOLLY. Well maybe it'd be better if the bold Stephen skipped his visit home this Christmas. (*Rises and turns her back on them.*) Jesus, misfortunes.

MARY *now wondering, concerned, her eyes on DOLLY's back, the stout figure.*

MOMMO. Yes. Misfortunes.

MARY. . . . Dolly?

DOLLY. Ooh, a cake, a candle – candles! what's the occasion? (*She gives a kiss to MOMMO.*) Well, I'm off now, darlin, an' God an' all his holy saints protect an' bless yeh.

MOMMO (*buried in her own thoughts until now*). When did you arrive?

DOLLY. What?

MOMMO. When did you arrive?

DOLLY. I arrived –

MOMMO. Sure you're welcome, when did you arrive?

DOLLY. I arrived –

MOMMO. Well did yeh?

DOLLY. I did.

MOMMO. From where?

DOLLY. From –

MOMMO. Now. And is that where y'are now?

DOLLY. The very location.

MOMMO. Now! I never knew that. Where?

DOLLY. Ahm . . . Aw Jesus, Mommo, you have us all as confused as yourself! Ballindine. Ball-in-dine.

MOMMO. Hah? Oh yes, yeh told me. Now. Who are you?

DOLLY. Dolly, I think.

MOMMO (*considering this, sucking her sweet*). Now. Dolly.

DOLLY. Dolly!

MOMMO. Yes.

DOLLY. Look, I have to be – (*going*). I'm Dolly, your granddaughter, and that's Mary, your other granddaughter, and your grandson Tom, Tom is dead.

MARY. Shh!

DOLLY. Ar, shh! (*To* MOMMO.) Now do you know?

MOMMO. I do. I'm waiting for someone.

DOLLY. Who're yeh waiting for?

MOMMO. I'm not tellin' yeh.

DOLLY. A man, is it?

MOMMO (*laughing*). 'Tis.

DOLLY. Och hona ho gus hah-haa, an' what'll he have for yeh!

MOMMO (*laughing*). A big stick.

DOLLY. M-m-m-m-m! – Stick, the bata! Mmmah! (*Sexual innuendo.*). Now! Try that subject on her if you want to stop her.

MOMMO. Oh but they were always after me.

DOLLY. An' did they ketch yeh?

MOMMO. The ones I wanted to.

DOLLY. An' are they still after yeh?

MOMMO. But I bolt the door – on some of them. (*Laughing.*)

DOLLY (*to MARY*). That's what all the aul ones like to talk about. I think you're goin' soft in the head.

MOMMO (*recognising her*). Is it Dolly? Aw is it my Dolly! Well, d'yeh know I didn't rec'nise yeh. Sure you were always the joker. Aw, my Dolly, Dolly, Dolly, come 'ere to me.

DOLLY *hesitates, is reluctant, then succumbs to the embrace; indeed, after a moment she is clinging tightly to the old woman.*

MARY *stands by, isolated, but watching the scene. She would love to be included. The smallest gesture of affection or recognition would help greatly.*

Ah, lovee. Lovee, lovee, lovee. Sure if I knew you were comin' – (*Aside to MARY.*) Will you put on the kettle, will you? Standing there! – I'd've baked a cake. That's an old one. Oh, mo pheata (*my pet*). Why didn't you send word? An' you got fat. You did! On me oath! Will you put on the kettle, Miss, will you! (*Whispering.*) Who is that woman?

DOLLY (*tearfully, but trying to joke*). She's the sly one.

MOMMO. She is. (*Loudly, hypocritically.*) Isn't she nice?

DOLLY. Watch her.

MARY *goes off to another room.*

MOMMO. Why is she interfering?

DOLLY. Shh, Mommo.

MOMMO. Be careful of that one.

DOLLY. I'm in terrible trouble.

MOMMO. Yes, watch her.

DOLLY (*extricating herself from the embrace, brushing away a tear*). Leave her to me. I'll deal with her. (*Calls.*) Miss! Will you come out, will you, an' make a brew! An' put something in it! Sure you should know about all kinds of potions.

MARY *has returned with a suitcase. She places it somewhere.*

. . . Someone going on a *voyage*?

MARY. I have to come to a decision, Dolly.

DOLLY. Again?

MARY. She's your responsibility too.

DOLLY. I know you think I inveigled you back here so that Stephen and I could escape.

MARY. No one inveigled me anywhere. You're not pulling your weight.

DOLLY (*shrugs*). There's always the County Home.

MARY. You –

DOLLY. Wouldn't I? Why should I stick myself again back in here?

MARY. Why should I?

DOLLY. In a place like this.

MARY. Why do I? In a place like this.

DOLLY (*shrugs*). That's your business. Well, I have to be going.

MARY. I'd like to go out sometimes too.

DOLLY. For a 'walk'? *Home*, I'm going.

MARY. You look it.

DOLLY. Alright. I'll tell you, so that you can go, where the man is waiting.

MARY. Man? *Men!*

  DOLLY *shrugs, is moving off.*

  I need to talk to – *someone!*

DOLLY (*her back to* MARY; *quietly*). I need to talk to someone too.

MARY (*an insinuation*). Why don't you take off your coat?

DOLLY (*faces* MARY; *a single solemn nod of her head; then*). Because, now, I am about to leave. I'll figure out something. I might even call back, 'cause it doesn't take long, does it? Just a few minutes; that's all it takes.

MARY. You're disgusting.

DOLLY. Am I?

MARY (*going to one of the other rooms*). I've *come* to a decision. (*Off.*) County Home! You won't blackmail me!

DOLLY (*to herself*). I hate this house. (*To* MOMMO.) Good man Josie! (*Going out; an undertone.*) Ah, fuck it all.

MOMMO. Oh yes. 'Good man, Josie!' Now! Good man Josie. And that was the second greeting Costello was to utter that evening.

MARY (*coming in*). I'll leave everything here for you spic and span, of course.

  She has not heard DOLLY *go out; now she stands there looking at the door, the motorcycle outside driving away, arms outstretched, her hands clapping together some of her wardrobe (as if demonstrating the possibility that she is leaving rather than confirming it).*

MOMMO. He got no reply. Nor did he expect one. For Josie was a Greaney and none was ever right in that fambly.

MARY (*to herself*). It's not fair.

MOMMO. An' the threadbare fashion'ry, not a top-coat to him, the shirt neck open.

MARY (*to herself*). Not a gansey.

MOMMO. Nor a gansey.

MARY. *Nor* a gansey. (*Calling after* DOLLY.) Stephen called me 'dearest'!

MOMMO. An' the tuthree raggedy top-coats on the others.

MARY. Wanted to have a child by me!

MOMMO. An' some with extra sacking bandaging around them.

MARY. A girl, he said, so that she'd look like me.

MOMMO. Though some say he had the knack of mendin' clocks, if he had.

MARY. But you'll never know a thing about it!

MOMMO. And none ever bested him at Ride-the-Blind-Donkey. (*She has a sip of tea.*) What's in this? Miss?

MARY. Your husband wined and dined and bedded me! (*Realising she has been talking to the door.*) I'm going soft in the head.

MOMMO. Miss!

MARY. The County Home! (*Gesturing, meaning did* MOMMO *hear what* DOLLY *said.*)

MOMMO. Hot drink, decent supa tea!

MARY (*automatically sets about making fresh tea, then she stops*). I have *come* to a decision I said. Do you understand? So if you could wait a moment. (*She starts to discard some of*

the clothes, packing others; talking to herself again.) Just to
see who is in earnest this time. I sit there —

MOMMO } Me mouth is dry d'ye know.
MARY } I just sit there. And I was doing well — I was the
success! Now I'm talking to myself. And I *will*
leave the place spic and span.

MOMMO. Howandever. 'How the boys!' was Costello's third
greeting. This time to two old men with their heads in the
chimbley, each minding a pint of black porter, before
Costello's coming in, they were in no need or hurry to be
drinkin'. The one of them givin' out the odd sigh, smoking his
pipe with assiduity and beating the slow obsequies of a death-
roll with his boot. An' the other, a Brian by name, replying in
sagacity 'Oh yis,' sharing the silent mysteries of the world
between them. Me mouth is (*dry*), d'ye know.

MARY. Just a moment! (*Going to another room.*) Dependent
on a pension and that bitch.

MOMMO. Where is she? Miss!

MARY (*off*). Miss! Miss is coming! (*Entering with more
clothes.*) Miss: as if I didn't exist. That's the thanks I get,
that's — (*Winces to herself.*) It's — not — thanks I'm looking
for. (*Absently.*) What am I looking for, Mommo? I had to
come home. No one inveigled me. I wanted to come home.

MOMMO. Put it down, put it down!

MARY. Why can't you be civil to me? At least tonight.

MOMMO. Put it down! (*She continues her story.*)

MARY, *exasperated, comes out of her reverie, dumps the
clothes and sets about making more tea.*

MARY. And you know very well who I am! You do! You do!

MOMMO. Sure it's often I'd be watchin' me own father
engaged in the same practice, drawing wisdom from the fire.
'Deed, on one such occasion, an' twas maybe after a full

hour's contemplation, he craned his neck, the glaze to his eyes, to accost me with the philosophy that was troublin' him. 'How much does a seagull weigh?' I held my silence to be sure, for times he'd get cross – oh he'd welt yeh with the stick – if a guess was attempted or a sound itself uttered. For he wouldn't be talkin' to you at all. The groans out of that man decipherin' the enigmal. Then, at last, when he found for himself the answer to the riddle he declared in 'sured solemnity, 'I'm thinking two ounces'. Now! That's who I'm waitin' for. Oh, men have their ways an' women their places an' that is God's plan, my bright ones.

She gets out of bed. MARY sees her and is hurrying to her assistance.

Shthap!

MARY is stopped by the ferocity. MOMMO squats, hidden behind the headboard of the bed.

MARY. . . . And to change your nightdress . . . I was a nurse, Mommo . . . And other offers of marriage . . . Plenty of them!

Then, quickly, she takes the opportunity of re-making the bed.

Wined and dined and bedded me. But I told him to keep away from me, to stop following me, to keep away from here.

She replaces the sheets with clean ones, removes the bed-warmer – which is a cast-iron lid of a pot in a knitted woollen cover; she puts the lid into the fire to reheat it. She appears almost happy when she is working constructively. She recites as she works.

'There is the silence of copse or croft
When the wind sinks dumb.
And of belfry loft
When the tenor after tolling stops its hum.'

And sure you have lots of poems, lots of stories, nice stories, instead of that old one. 'Mick Delaney' – Do you remember that one? We loved that one. How did it begin? Or ghost stories. People used to come *miles* to hear you tell stories. Oh! And do you remember: the gramophone? Yes, we had a gramophone too. 'The banshee is out tonight go down (*on*) your knees and say your prayers – Wooooo!' Or would you like me to read you a story?

MOMMO (*reappearing from behind the bed*). Heh heh heh heh!

MARY (*now her solemn grave face*). There was happiness here too, Mommo. Harmony?

MOMMO (*straight back, neck craned*). You can be going now, Miss.

MARY. . . . Alright.

She takes the chamberpot from behind the headboard of the bed and goes out. We can see her outside, motionless; a little later, continuing motionless except for the movements of smoking a cigarette.

MOMMO. She knows too much about our business entirely. (*She calls hypocritically.*) And thank you! (*Giggles getting back into the bed.*) Now amn't I able for them? (*Sings.*) 'Once I loved with fond affection, all my thoughts they were in thee, till a dork (*dark*) haired girl deceived me –' Ye like that one.
   But now that Costello was in it the aspect was transforming. 'An',' says old Brian, taking his head out of the fire, 'what's the news from the Big World?' 'The Dutch has taken Holland!' says Costello with such a rumble out of him near had the whole house shook asunder and all in it in ululation so infectious was the sound. Save Josie who was heedless, but rapping with severity on the counter for more libation. And 'John!' says the young buxom woman, calling to her husband – 'John!' – to come out and tend his end of the counter, an' she now putting questions on bold Costello.
   'You wor in Tuam?' says she, 'I was in Tuam,' says he.

'Yeh wor?' says she. 'I was,' says he. 'An' how was it?' says she.

'Well, not tellin' you a word of a lie now,' says he 'but 'twas deadly'.

And 'Ory!' says the crone that was in it buyin' the salt.

'Did yeh hear?' says the young buxom woman to her husband. John, to be sure. He had 'rived from the kitchen an' was frownin' pullin' pints. Merchants d'ye know: good market or bad, the arithmetic in the ledger has to come out correct. An' the multifarious diversifications in matters of local commerce, the head had to be working perpetually.

'Well do yeh tell me so?' says the young buxom woman.

'I do tell yeh so,' says Costello. 'Talkin' about a Maragadh Mór? – I never in all me born days seen light or likes of it!'

Now they were listening.

MARY *comes in, washes and replaces the chamberpot. She selects her 'going-away' suit from the second bundle of clothes which she brought from the other room and, trying the waist against herself, she puts the suit on a chair beside the fire to air it. She leaves her clothes to go out twice through the following and bring in two armsful of turf.*

MOMMO. 'Firkins of butter,' says he, 'an' cheese be the hundred-weight. Ducks, geese, chickens, bonavs and – Geese!' says he, 'geese! There was hundreds of them! There was hundreds upon hundreds of thousands of them! The ground I tell ye was white with them!'

And 'White with them,' says the crone.

'They went ch-cheap then?' says John, still bowed frownin' over the tricks of pullin' porter.

'Cheap then?' says Costello, 'sure yeh couldn't give them away sure. Sure the sight of so many chickens an' geese an'! Sure all the people could do was stand and stare.'

'They were puzzled,' says the crone.

'I'm tellin' ye,' says Costello, 'Napoleon Bonaparte wouldn't have said no to all the provisions goin' a-beggin' in that town of Tuam today.'

An' 'Hah?' says John, squintin', the head-work interrupted.

'On his retreat from Moscow, sure,' says Costello. 'Or Josephine – Wuw! – neither.'

Now! Wuw. Them were his ways, an' he off rumblin' again: 'Oh, I'm a bold bachelor aisy an' free, both city and country is aiqual to me!' having the others equivalently pursuant: 'Wo ho ho, wo ho ho!'

'But you sis-sold the rabbits, d-did yeh, Costello?' says John. An' wasn't there a gap. Oh, only for the second. 'Oh I sold them,' then sayin' Costello. 'Oh I did, did,' saying he. 'Oh on me solemn 'n dyin' oath! Every man-jack-rabbit of them.' Like a man not to be believed, his bona fides in question.

'Yeh-yeh c-odjer yeh-yeh,' says John. Whatever he meant. But he was not at all yet feeling cordial.

But thus was the night faring into its progression, others 'riving back home an' how did they do an' who else was in it, did they buy e'er a thing, Costello settin' them laughin', John frownin' an' squintin', an' the thief of a Christmas they wor all goin' t'have. What're ye doin' there?

MARY *is stacking the turf near the fire. She holds up a sod of turf to show* MOMMO.

Hah? . . . There's nothing here for people to be prying in corners for.

MARY *holds up the woollen cover of the bed-warmer.*

Hah? . . . Bring in the brishen of turf an' then you may be goin' home to your own house.

MARY. . . . Alright.

She moves as if going out back door, then moves silently to the comparative dark of the far corner of the room where she remains motionless.

MOMMO. You couldn't be up to them.

MARY *continues silent. She is trying a new ploy, hoping* MOMMO *will stop, will sleep.*

Isn't life a strange thing too? 'Tis. An' if we could live it
again? . . . Would we? (*live it differently*) In harmony? Aah, I
don't know. (*She yawns.*) Oh ho huneo! An' 'twas round
about now the rattlin' of the horse an' cart was heard
evidential abroad an' had them peepin' at the windy. 'Twas
the decent man an' his decent wife the same was in it. And
'Stand, Pedlar,' says the man in (*a*) class of awesome whisper.
And his decent wife from the heel of the cart to his side to
view the spectre was now before them. The aspect silver of
moon an' stars reflecting off the new impossibility.
Loughran's Hill. Creature. She now clutching more tightly the
sweets to her breast. Switch off that aul' thing (*the radio*),
there's nothing on it. (*She yawns again: her eyes close.*)

They were silent a while.

MARY (*whispers*). Sleep.

MOMMO (*eyes open*). Hah? (*Looking around.*) Now what was
there for doing? Which way to cast the hopeful eye. No-no,
not yet, in deliberate caution, would he acknowledge the
shop, John Mah'ny's, forninst them. But looked behind him
the road they came, forward again, but to what avail? There
was only John Mah'ny's now for his deep contemplation,
nature all around them serenely waiting, and didn't the two
little smiles come appearing again.

MOMMO *slides a little down the bed.*

MARY (*whispers*). Sleep.

MOMMO. Hah?

MARY. Sleep, sleep. Peace, peace.

MOMMO (*yawns*). An' the strangers, that decent man an' his
decent wife the same, were rounding the gable into the
merchant's yard, an' sorry the night that was the decision.
What time is it? . . . She's gone. An' she can stay gone. But
them are the details, c'rrect to the particular. And they can be
vouched for. For there was to be many's the inquisition by
c'roner, civic guard and civilian on all that transpired in John

Mah'ny's that night. Now. Wasn't that a nice story? An' we'll all be goin' to sleep.

She is asleep.

Tommy O'Brien's programme is over (or nearly over): it is followed by an announcement of what The Sunday Concert *is going to be later on: 'A Shubert Evening, Symphony No. 9, 'The Great', followed by 'Notturno' in E Flat. But now we have* Archives *presented by . . .' etc.*

MARY *continues motionless for some moments.*

A car passes by outside.

MARY (*looking at* MOMMO). Sleep?
For how long? . . .

She switches off the radio. She switches off the light. She goes to the table and idly starts lighting three or four of the candles on the cake, using a new match to light each successive candle.

(*To herself:*) Give me my freedom, Mommo . . . What freedom? . . . No freedom without structure . . . Where can I go? . . . How can I go (*Looking up and around at the rafters.*) with all this? (*She has tired of her idle game of lighting the candles.*) . . . And it didn't work before for me, did it? . . . I came back.
  (*To herself, and idly at first:*) Now as all do know . . . Now as all do know . . . Now as all do know the world over the custom when entering the house of another — be the house public, private with credentials or no — is to invoke our Maker's benediction on all present. (*Adds a piece of sardonic humour:*) Save the cat. Well, as the Bailegangaires would have it later, no mention of our Maker, or His Blessed Son, was mentioned as the strangers came 'cross that threshel (*threshold*). But no, no, no, no, no. No now! They were wrongin' that couple. (*To the sleeping* MOMMO.) Weren't they? They wor. They were. (*To* MOMMO.) And when you.

And when that decent woman gave the whole story to her father, what did he say? (*A touch of mimicry of* MOMMO.) An' believe you me he knew all about them. That the Bailegangaires were a venomous pack of jolter-headed gobshites. Didn't he? He did. Now for yeh! An ill-bred band of amadáns an' oinseachs, untutored in science, philosophy or the fundamental rudimentaries of elementary husbandry itself. A low crew of illiterate plebs, drunkards and incestuous bastards, and would ever continue as such – (*Holds up her finger to correct her wording.*) and would ever continue as *much*, improper and despicable in their incorrigibility. Them were his words. Weren't they? They wor. They're not nice, he said. Supa tea. (*Short sardonic laugh as she pours a glass of vodka for herself.*) And he was the man to give the tongue-lashin'. An' 'twas from him I got my learnin'. Wasn't it? That's who I'm waitin' for. (*She has a sip of the vodka.*) Too sweet. (*She dilutes the vodka with water.*) Me father. He has a big stick. That's where security lies. (*She has a drink: then, whimpering as* MOMMO *might.*) I wanta go home, I wanta go home. (*New tone, her own, frustrated.*) So do I, so do I. Home. (*Anger.*) Where is it, Mommo?

Then she is sorry for her anger. She pulls herself together for a few moments. The silence is now being punctuated by a car passing by outside.

A lot of activity tonight. And all weekend.

MARY *picks up her book and does not open it.*

'There is the silence of copse or croft.'

She starts to pace the periphery of the room.

'When the wind sinks dumb.
And of belfry loft
When the tenor after tolling stops its hum.

And there's the silence of a lonely pond
Where a man was drowned . . .'

She stops for a moment or two looking at one of the framed photographs.

Where a man, and his brother who went to save him . . . were drowned. Bury them in pairs, it's cheaper.

Continues pacing.

'Nor high nor yond
No newt, toad, frog to make the smallest sound.

But the silence of an empty house
Where oneself was born,
Dwelt, held carouse . . .'

   Did we? Hold carouse.

'With friends
Is of all silence most forlorn.

It seems no power can waken it –'

Another car passes by. MARY's *reaction to the car.*

Come in! 'Or rouse its rooms,
Or the past permit
The present to stir a torpor like a tomb's.'

Bla bla bla bla bla, like a tomb's. (*To the book, and dumping it.*) Is that so? Well, I don't agree with you . . . What time is it? Twenty past nine . . . Going crazy. (*Then, on reflection.*) No I'm not. (*Then suddenly to* MOMMO.) Wake up *now*, Mommo. Mommo! Because I don't want to wait till midnight, or one or two or three o'clock in the morning, for more of your – unfinished symphony. I'm ready *now*. (*She switches on the light.*) Mommo, the curséd paraffin! (*She switches on the radio.*) What else did your father say when you gave him the story? That many's the one's son or daughter married into that place went mental after and had to be took away, sullyin' and bringin' disgrace on a line that had been clean up to then, maybe both sides! What else did he say? (MOMMO *is awake*.) What about the snails? What about the earwigs?

MOMMO. 'Oh never step on a snail,' he intoned.

MARY. 'Nor upon the silver trail he leaves behind.'

MOMMO. 'For your boot is unworthy.'

MARY. Now!

MOMMO. 'For the snail knows his place,' he groaned, 'and understands the constant parameters – and the need for parameters – in the case under consideration, God's prize piece, the earth. And therefore the snail is free, and all he does is in innocence.' He did.

MARY. On with the story.

MOMMO. 'D'yeh consider,' says he – the fierce eyes of that man rolling – 'that God designed all this for the likes of the gobshite Bochtáns and their antics?'

MARY. Or for the likes of ourselves?

MOMMO. Or for the likes of ourselves. He did. Them wor his words. That's who I'm waitin' for.

MARY. To continue. But that decent man and his decent wife the same did as was proper on entering.

MOMMO. Sure we weren't meant to be here at all!

MARY. The customary salutation was given.

MOMMO. That was one of God's errors.

MARY. Though silently, for they were shy people, and confused in their quandry. Mommo? And then, without fuss, the man indicated a seat in the most private corner.

MOMMO. An' they were wrongin' them there again! So they wor.

MARY. They were.

MOMMO. They wor. The whispers bein' exchanged were *not* of malevolent disposition. Yis! – to be sure! – that woman! – Maybe! – had a distracted look to her. Hadn't she reason?

MARY. The Bailegangaires gawpin' at them.

MOMMO. They knew no better.

MARY. Where would they learn it?

MOMMO. Oh-ho, but he bet them – Och hona ho gus hah-haa! he bet the best of them! . . . Incestuous bastards. (*Absently asking*) Cigarette. 'An' I caught Tom playin' with the mangler the other evenin', his feet dancin' in the cup.' That's what she was whisperin'. And he lookin' round, 'Not at all, not at all,' tryin' to look pleasant in the house of another. 'An' won't they have to light the lamp?' That's what she was whisperin'. 'Not at all, not at all,' still lookin' for the place to put his eyes. 'Isn't Mary a big girl now an' well able to look after them.' That's what he was whisperin'. 'An' won't May Glynn be lookin' in on them.' That's what he was whisperin'. But she'd told May Glynn that mornin' not to be waitin', her mother'd be needin' her to look after her young brothers, an' they'd be home before dark for sure. And-sure-she-was-gettin'-on-his-nerves! Till he had to go an' leave her there to a quiet spot at the counter . . . Sure she should've known better. An' she's sorry now. She is. She is. (*Whimpering.*) I wanta see mah father.

MARY *coming to comfort her.*

Shtap! . . . (*Whimpering.*) I wanta go home. (*Warning* MARY; *at the same time taking the cigarette which* MARY *is offering her.*) And he has a big stick.

MARY. I'm not trying to stop you, Mommo.

MOMMO. An' he won't try to stop me. Heh heh heh heh. (*She puffs at the cigarettte and then winks wisely at the imagined children at the foot of the bed.*) Men long-married to tearful women are no use to them, my bright ones. But are apt to get

cross, and make matters worse, when they can't see the
solution. (*She becomes aware of the cigarette.*) What's this?
An' who asked for this?

MARY (*taking cigarette from her*). I'm not stopping you. And I
just had an idea.

MOMMO ⎱ Me mouth is burned.
MARY ⎰ We'll do it together.

Speaking simultaneously:

MOMMO. Rubbishy cigarettes – spendin' money on rubbishy
cigarettes –

MARY. We'll finish it. What is it but an old auld story? I'm not
stopping you –

MOMMO (*singing: her defiance to* MARY). 'Once I loved with
fond affection –'

MARY. And if we finished it, that would be something at least,
wouldn't it?

MOMMO. 'All my thoughts they were in thee.'

MARY. Wouldn't it?

MOMMO. 'And no more he thought of me.' (*She lapses into
silence, she grows drowsy, or feigns drowsiness.*)

MARY (*singing*). 'Tooralloo ralloo ralladdy, tooralloo ralloo
rallee, till a dark – (*Corrects herself.*) *dork* haired girl
deceived me, and no more thought of me' . . . I'll help you,
Mommo.

MOMMO. Tom is in Galway. He's afeared of the gander.

MARY. Don't go to sleep. and don't be pretending to sleep
either. And what'll you be havin', says John Mahony the
proprietor. But the stranger was now puzzlin' something in

his brain, he taking in the laughter and Costello's great
bellow dominating over all.

'A lotta noise an' little wool as the devil says shearin' the
pig!' sayin' Costello. Wo ho ho! 'An what'll you be havin',
Mister,' says John Mahony again. 'A little drop of whiskey
an' a small port wine.' And readying the drinks up above,
says John, 'The frost is determined to make a night of it?'
Says he.

'Behell I don't know,' says old Brian, like the nestor long
ago, 'comin' on duskess there was a fine roll of cloud over in
the west and if you got the bit of a breeze at all I'm thinkin'
you'd soon see a thaw.' And the stranger had produced his
purse and was suspended-paused takin' in the forecast. But
the two little smiles appearing again, the compendium of his
deliberations was that such good fortune as a thaw was not
to be. Then – and with a deft enough flick – he pitched the
coin on the counter – like a man rejecting all fortune. Good
enough.

He took the drink to his decent wife and was for sitting
next to her again but wasn't her head now in and out of the
corner and she startin' the cryin'.

MOMMO. She should have known better.

MARY. So what could he do but leave her there again?

MOMMO. An' the church owed him money.

MARY. Did it?

MOMMO (growls). The-church-owed-him-money. Oh, the
church is slow to pay out. But if you're givin', there's nothin'
like money to make them fervent! There's nothin' like money
t'make the clergy devout.

MARY. Yes?

MOMMO (drowsily). And I'm thinkin' that decent man of late
was given to reviewin' the transpirations since his birth . . .
But if he was itself, wasn't his decent wife the same? . . . At
the end of her tether . . . They were acquainted with grief . . .

They wor . . . They wor. Switch off that aul' thing (*the radio*) . . . They wor.

MARY. . . . Mommo? (*She has turned the volume down a bit.*) I know you're pretending, Mommo?

The silence again.

They were acquainted with grief . . . Alright, I won't just help you, I'll do it for you. (*Progressively she begins to dramatise the story more.*) Now John Mahony, (*She corrects her pronunciation.*) Now John Mah'ny was noticing the goings-on between the two and being the proprietor he was possessed of the licence for interrogating newses. And 'you have a distance to go, Mister?' says he. (*Corrects herself again.*) 'You have a d-distance teh-teh g-go, *Mister*?' says he at the stranger. An' says Grandad. An' says the stranger, class of frownin'. 'Would that big man down there,' says he, 'be a man by the name of Costello?' And, 'Th-that's who he is,' says John, 'D'yeh know him?' 'No,' says the stranger, in curious introspection, an' 'No' says he again – *still* puzzled in the head. But that's a fine laugh.' 'Oh 'tis a f-fine laugh right enough,' says John, 'Hah?' Knowin' more was comin' but hadn't yet reached the senses. And the stranger now drawin' curlicues with his glass upon the counter! Then says he, 'I heard that laugh a wintry day two years ago across the market square in Ballindine an' I had t'ask a man who he was.' 'Yeh had,' says John. 'I had,' says the stranger, still drawin' the curlicues an' now admiring his own artistry. An' John was in suspense. And then, of a suddenness, didn't the frown go disappearin' up the stranger's cap. He had it at last. 'Well,' says he – Oh, lookin' the merchant between the two eyes, 'Well,' says he, 'I'm a better laugher than your Costello.'

What time is it? Half-nine. *Someone* will come yet. '*Nother* supa milk (*Short laugh to herself as she gets another glass of vodka.*) Well, I'm a better laugher than your Costello. (*She swallows the drink.*) Now the merchant betrayed nothing. He was well-versed in meeting company, an' all he did was nod the once – (*She nods.*) and then, quick enough of him,

referred the matter. And Sh-Sheamus!' says he, 'Sh-sh-
Sheamus!' callin' Costello to come down.

*She is now listening to the 'putt-putt' of the motorcycle
approaching.*

A mortal laughing competition there would be.

MARY *now into action, putting away her glass, switching off
the radio, getting needle, thread, scissors and the skirt of her
'going-away' suit to take in the waist.*

I knew some one would call. Dolly. Again! I wonder why.
(*Cynically.*) Bringing tidings of great joy.

MARY *is seated by the fire.*

DOLLY *comes in. She stretches herself. (She has had her sex
in ditch, doorway, old shed or wherever.) She takes in the
packed suitcase but as usual leaves such baiting topics until it
suits her.*

DOLLY. I have it all figured out.

MARY. The County Home?

DOLLY. Well, maybe nothing as drastic as that. That's a nice
suit.

MARY (*does not lift her head from her work*). Kill her?

DOLLY (*a sideways twist of the head – 'Kill her?' – a more
feasible suggestion*). Can I have a drop of this? (*vodka*)

MARY. You brought it.

DOLLY (*produces two bottles of mixers*). I forgot the mixers
earlier. In my haste. (*She pours two drinks.*) We might as well
have a wake, an American wake for yeh.

MARY. Not for me. I had a little one earlier, thank you.

DOLLY. You had *two* little ones, (*Puts drink beside* MARY.) Vodka and white. It's a long time since I seen you wearing that.

MARY. Saw.

DOLLY. What?

MARY. I wore it coming home.

DOLLY. Did you have to let out the waist?

MARY. I have to take *in* my things. (*A gesture of invitation.*) You need to talk to someone.

DOLLY. Go on: cheers! Since you're off. Are yeh?

MARY (*does not drink, does not look up but lifts her glass and puts it down again*). Cheers!

DOLLY. And it often crossed my mind the years Stephen and I were here with herself. Kill her. And it wouldn't be none of your fancy nurses' potions either. Get them out of bed, the auld reliable, start them walkin'. Walk the heart out of them. No clues left for coroner or Dr Paddy. And that's how many's the one met their Waterloo. What's the matter?

MARY *shakes her head; just when she does not want to, she is about to break into tears.*

. . . What? . . . Joking . . . I have it all figured out.

MARY *is crying.*

What's the matter?

MARY. Stop it, Dolly.

DOLLY. Mary?

MARY. Leave me alone. (*To get away from* DOLLY *she goes to the radio and switches it on.*) Leave me alone.

DOLLY. What's the . . . Why are you . . . (*She emits a few whimpers.*) Mary?

MOMMO (*has woken up and is watching them suspiciously*).
Heh heh heh heh.

DOLLY. Good man Josie! (*And immediately back to* MARY.)
Mary? Why are you? Don't.

MOMMO. What's the plottin' an' whisperin' for?

DOLLY. Good man Josie! (*And immediately back to* MARY
again.) What? (*Crying.*) What? . . . Don't. Please. (*Her arms
around* MARY.)

They are all speaking at once. MARY *and* DOLLY *crying*.

MOMMO. Oh yes, 'Good man, Josie.' Now! Good man, Josie.
And that was the second greeting he uttered that night.

DOLLY. What? . . . Shh! . . . What?

MARY. I don't know, I don't know.

MOMMO. He got no reply. Nor did he expect one. For Josie
was a Greaney, an' none was ever right in that fambly.

MARY. I wanted to come home.

DOLLY. What?

MARY. I had to come home.

MOMMO. An' the threadbare fashion'ry, not a top-coat to
him, the shirt neck open, nor a gansey.

DOLLY. What?

MARY. This is our home.

DOLLY. I know.

MARY. This is our home.

DOLLY. I know.

MARY (*pulling away from* DOLLY *to shout at* MOMMO.)
Finish it, finish it, that much at least —

MOMMO. Och hona ho gus hah-haa!

MARY. Have done with it! – that much at least!

MOMMO. Och hona ho gus hah-haa!

MARY (*to* DOLLY *who is following her*). Why don't you take
off your coat! (*To* MOMMO.) What was waiting for them at
dawn when they got home in the morning?

MARY's *remark to* DOLLY *has stopped* DOLLY *for a
moment, but* DOLLY *comes to* MARY *and puts her arms
around her again, the two of them crying through to the end.
And* MOMMO *has not given way to the above, continuing
without pause.*

MOMMO. Wo ho ho! Heh heh heh! Wo ho ho! – Heh heh
heh! – An' the tuthree raggedy top-coats on the others! – The
poor an' neglected, the wretched an' forlorn – 'Twas the best
night ever! – the impoverished an' hungry, eyes big as
saucers, howlin' their defiance at the heavens through the
ceilin' – Och hona ho gus hah-haa! – inviting of what else
might come or care to come! Wo ho ho – Heh heh heh . . .
(*Quietening down.*) Though some say he had the knack of
mendin' clocks, if he had. And none ever bested him at Ride-
the-Blind-Donkey. Howandever. 'How the boys!' was
Costello's third greeting, this time to two old men with their
heads in the chimbley . . .

*The lights fading through the above and music up —
'Notturno'.*

ACT TWO

*'Notturno', introducing Act Two, fades under the
announcement for* The Sunday Concert *on the radio together
with* MOMMO's *voice continuing her story.* MOMMO *has
arrived at and is repeating the last section of the story where*
MARY *left off in Act One.*

A sniff from MARY, *her tears are all but finished. Both she
and* DOLLY *have their 'vodkas and white' and a slice of the
birthday cake on plates beside them.* MARY *is examining a
small computerised gadget*

MOMMO. . . . 'yeh had', says John. 'I had' says the stranger,
still drawin' the curlicues an' admiring his own artistry.

MARY. What is it? (*the gadget*)

DOLLY. I don't know. Happy birthday!

MOMMO. An' John was in suspense. An' then of a suddenness
didn't the frown go disappearing up the stranger's cap. He
had it at last.

MARY. It's not a calculator.

DOLLY. Data processing thing from the plant above.

MARY. You didn't get a handbook?

DOLLY. I got it off one of the lads, working in the – You're the
brainy one.

MOMMO. 'Well,' says he – oh lookin' the merchant between
the two eyes – 'Well,' says he, 'I'm a better laugher than your
Costello.'

DOLLY. Give it to her if you like.

MARY. No. (*It is precious; a present.*) I'm sorry for. (*Crying.*)

A car passes by outside.

DOLLY. Ar — Phhh — don't be silly. Did yeh see the helicopter on Friday? The plant, they say, is for closure. The Chinese are over.

MARY. Japanese, (*Her attention now returning to* MOMMO.)

MOMMO. Now the merchant betrayed nothing.

DOLLY. I prefer to call them Chinese. (*Watching* MARY *go to* MOMMO.)

DOLLY's *mind beginning to tick over on how to present her 'proposition' to* MARY. MARY's *nervous energy, after the lull, setting her to work again, washing her plate, removing the bed-warmer from the fire and slipping it into the bed at* MOMMO's *feet, wrapping up the cake in tinfoil and putting it away, stoking the fire . . . but, predominantly, her eyes, concentration, always returning to* MOMMO; *a resoluteness increasing to have* MOMMO's *story finished.*

MOMMO. He was well-versed at meeting company. And all he did was nod the once. (*She nods solemnly.*)

DOLLY. I must get a set of decent glasses for you the next time I'm in town.

MOMMO. Then, quick enough of him, referred the matter.

DOLLY. And I'm sure there's rats in that thatch.

MOMMO. An' 'Sh-Sheamus!' says he.

DOLLY. I could see Hallilan the contractor about slatin' it.

MOMMO. 'Sh-Sheamus!' Calling Costello to come down.

DOLLY. What d'yeh think?

MARY. Shhh!

MOMMO. A laughing competition there would be.

DOLLY (*puzzled by* MARY's *behaviour*). And I was thinking of getting her a doll.

MARY (*her eyes fastened on* MOMMO). No, let's see if she'll continue.

DOLLY. What?

MARY. Good enough. Then down steps the bold Costello.

MOMMO. Pardon? (*And instead of continuing she starts singing.*) 'Once I loved with fond affection, all my thoughts they were in thee, till a dork haired gurl deceived me, and no more he thought of me.'

MARY (*through* MOMMO's *song, returning to the fire, all the time looking at* MOMMO). Down steps the bold Costello. You have some suggestion, something figured out.

DOLLY. What?

MARY. She's going to finish it.

DOLLY. Finish it? Why?

MARY. I don't know. I can't do anything the way things are.

MOMMO. Now. Ye like that one.

DOLLY. I thought you were trying to stop her. Sit down.

MARY. She's going to finish it.

DOLLY. You're always on your feet —

MARY. *Tonight!*

DOLLY. I want to have a chat. Another drink?

MARY (*mechanically about to pour drinks, stops*). No. A laughing competition there *will* be! (*And goes to* MOMMO.) Then down steps the bold Costello.

MOMMO. Pardon?

MARY. Then down steps the bold Costello.

MOMMO. Oh yes.

DOLLY. Well, as a matter of fact, I do have a proposition.

MARY. Shhh!

MOMMO. Then down steps the bold Costello. And 'Hah?' says he, seeing the gravity on the proprietor's mien. But the proprietor – John, to be sure – referred him like that (*She nods in one direction.*) An 'Hah?' says Costello, lookin' at the stranger. But weren't the two eyes of the stranger still mildly fixed on John, an' 'Hah?' says Costello, lookin' back at John. But there was no countin' John's cuteness. He takes the two steps backwards, then the one step to the sidewards, slidin' his arse along the shelf to 'scape the strangers line of vision an' demonstrate for all his neutrality in the matter. 'Hah!' poor Costello goin'. 'Hah!' to the one, 'Hah!' to the other. 'Hah?' 'Hah?' The head swung near off his neck, an' now wonderin' I'm sure what on earth he'd done wrong – 'Hah!' – an' 'twas a bailey in disguise maybe was the small little stranger. Costello was a delightful poacher.

DOLLY. Mary? (*Topping up the drinks.*)

MOMMO. An' no help from John. Puffing a tuneless whistle at the ceiling!

DOLLY. I have a proposition.

MOMMO. 'Phuh-phuh-phuh-phuh.'
(*John's tuneless whistle.*)

MARY (*absently accepting drink*). Phuh-phuh-phuh-phuh.

MOMMO. Then says the stranger –

DOLLY (*to herself*). Jesus!

MOMMO. His eyes now mild, lookin' straight ahead at nothing –

DOLLY. She's (MARY) gone loopey too.

MARY. Good girl.

MOMMO. Though 'twas polite introduction – 'How d'yeh do, Mr Costello, I'm Seamus O'Toole'. Costello: 'Hah! I'm very well, thanking you!' His face was a study, 'An' 'Oh,' says John of Costello, 'He's a Sh-Sheamus too, phuh-phuh-phuh-phuh.' 'I know that,' says the stranger, 'but I'm a better

laugher than 'm.' 'Kuhaa, uck-uck-uck-khuck, kuh-haa a
haa!' In Costello's throat. In response didn't the stranger
make serious chuckle. And in response to that didn't Costello
roar out a laugh.

A silent 'Jesus' from DOLLY. *She decides to take off her coat
and see what effect flaunting her pregnancy will have.*

MARY *speaking simultaneously/silently with* MOMMO.

MARY (*silently with* MOMMO). Then loud as you
please . . . . .

MOMMO. Then loud as you please says Costello: 'He says, he
says, he says,' says he, 'he's a better.' (*She claps her mouth
shut.*) An' that was far as he got. For in the suddenness of a
discovery he found out that he was cross.
    'Ara phat?' says he – He was nimble? – The full size of him
skippin' backwards, the dancing antics of a boxing-man. An'
lookin' 'bout at his supporters, now hushed an' on their
marks, 'He says, he says, he says,' says he, 'he's a better
laugher than me!'
    What! Sure they never heard the likes. Nor how on earth to
deal with it. An' the upset on their own man's face! – Oh,
they wor greatly taken 'back. They wor. Oh they wor. An'
not up to dissertation things wor lookin' dangerous.

DOLLY. She's getting tired – the creature.

MARY. Shhh!

DOLLY. Cheers!

MARY. Cheers – Things were looking dangerous.

MOMMO. They were. Oh, they wor.

MARY. 'Ary give me (*a*) pint outa that.'

MOMMO. Costello?

    MARY *nods.*

Swivellin' an' near knockin' them wor behind him, but then
in retraction comes wheelin' back 'round, the head like a
donkey's flung up at the ceilin', eyes like a bull-frog's near out

the sockets an' the big mouth threwn open. But God bless us an' save us, all the emission was (a) class of a rattle'd put shame to a magpie.

MARY (*silently, excited*). Shame to a magpie.

MOMMO. Now he was humbled, the big head on him hangin', went back to his corner, turned his back on all present – The hump that was on him! Oh his feelin's wor hurted. (*She yawns.*) Oh ho hun-neo.

MARY. Aa no.

MOMMO (*insistent*). Oh ho hun-neo!

MARY. Don't be pretendin', you had a little nap a while ago.

MOMMO. Put the sup of milk there for me now for the night.

MARY. I'll get the milk later. And the others, Mommo?

MOMMO. Lookin' wildly, one to the other, from their giant to the stranger, none knowin' what to do.

DOLLY (*getting the milk*). Let her settle down.

MARY. But they were vexed.

MOMMO. An' they knew it?

MARY *nods agreement and encouragement.*

Oh they knew they were cross. An' strainin' towards the stranger like mastiffs on chains, fit to tear him asunder.

DOLLY. And I don't know if you've noticed, Mary, but the turf out there won't last the winter. (*Approaching with the milk.*) Here we are! I'll see to the turf.

MARY (*takes the milk from* DOLLY). No milk.

DOLLY. What are you at?

MARY. No milk! (*She puts it away.*)

MOMMO. And even Josie! – the odd one –

DOLLY (*to herself*). Jesus Josie! –

MOMMO. That always stood aloof! Even he was infected with the venom (*that*) had entered, an' all of the floor was 'vailable round him he began to walk circles screechin' 'Hackah!' at the stranger.

DOLLY. I want to have a talk!

MARY. Later.

DOLLY. A plan, a proposition.

MARY. Later.

MOMMO. Pardon?

DOLLY. And I've a little problem of my own.

MARY. I think I've noticed. Go on, Mommo, no one is stopping you.

MOMMO. Where's the milk for the night, Miss?

MARY. Then striding to the stranger – Costello: 'Excuse me there now a minute, Mister –'

DOLLY. Mary –

MARY. No! No! 'Excuse me there now a minute now –'

MOMMO. Pardon?

MARY. 'But what did you say to me there a minute ago?' (*Waits for a beat to see if* MOMMO *will continue.*) . . . 'That you're a better laugher than me, is it?' . . . 'Well, would you care to put a small bet on it?'

MOMMO (*suspiciously, but childlike*). How do you know that?

MARY. Oh, I was told. But I never heard all of the story.

MOMMO. Hah? . . . Ar shurrup (*shut up*) outa that.

MARY. 'Well would you care to put a small bet on it?' And 'No', saying the stranger going back to his wife. 'But you're challenging me, challenging me, challenging me, y'are!'

MOMMO. 'No', saying the stranger. ''twas only a notion,' his eyes on the floor. For why? Forseeing fatalistic danger. (MARY *nods solemnly*.) Then joined the two little smiles cross the width of his mouth which he gave up to the hero as evidence sincere that he was for abnegating. Can yeh go on?

MARY. No. (*Cajoling*.) Can you?

MOMMO. Well, Costello was for agreein'? An' for understandin'? But th' others wor all circlin', jostlin', an' pushin' – Josie flailin' like a thrasher – eggin' for diversion, 'He is, he is, challe'gin' yeh, he is!' 'Up Bochtán, up Bochtán, Bochtán forever!' Putting confusion in the head of Costello again. But the stranger – a cute man – headin' for the door, gives (*the*) nod an' wink to Costello so he'd comprehend the better the excitation (*that*) is produced by the abberation of a notion. Then in the fullness of magistrature, 'Attention!' roaring Costello, 'Attention!' roaring he, to declare his verdict was dismissal, an' decree that 'twas all over.

MARY. Yes?

MOMMO. An' 'twas.

MARY. Aa, you have more for me?

MOMMO (*childlike*). Have I?

MARY *nods*. MOMMO *thinking her own thoughts, then she shakes her head*.

MARY. A laughing competition there would be.

MOMMO (*absently*). A what?

DOLLY. She's exhausted.

MARY. She's not!

MOMMO. Where was I? . . . The jostlin' an' pushin' . . . (*Then her eyes searching the floor, in half-memory, lamenting trampled sweets*.) The sweets.

MARY. Here they are. (*The ones that DOLLY brought*.)

MOMMO. The sweets (*Rejecting the sweets, her eyes still searching the floor.*) In the jostlin' an' pushin' . . . The sweets for her children trampled under their boots.

MARY. Here they are, under your pillow.

MOMMO (*takes them absently*). Hahum?

DOLLY. Can't you see she's —

MARY. She's not.

MOMMO. Phuh: dust.

DOLLY. And you're worn out too, Mary.

MARY. But if Costello decreed 'twas all over, how did it start?

MOMMO. How did? The small stranger, I told yeh, goin' out to check the weather for as had been forecasted the thaw was settling in.

MARY. I see!

MOMMO. An' sure they could have got home.

MARY. Yes?

MOMMO. They could have got home. (*Brooding, growls; then.*) Costello could decree. All others could decree. (*Quiet anger.*) But what about the things had been vexin' *her* for years? No, a woman isn't stick or stone. The forty years an' more in the one bed together an' he to rise in the mornin' (and) not to give her a glance. An' so long it had been he had called her by first name, she'd near forgot it herself . . . Brigit . . . Hah? . . . An' so she thought he hated her . . . An' maybe he did, like everything else . . . An'. (*Her head comes up, eyes fierce.*) Yis, yis-yis, he's challe'gin' ye, he is!' She gave it to the Bochtáns. And to her husband returning? — maybe he would recant, but she'd renege matters no longer. 'Och hona ho gus hah-haa' — she hated him too.

MARY *leans back; she has not heard this part of the story before.*

MARY. . . . And what happened then?

MOMMO. An' what happened then. Tried to pacify her. (*Growls.*) But there-was-none-would-assuage-her. An' what happened then, an' what happened then. 'Stand up then,' says Costello. They already standin'. 'Scath siar uaim' to the rest to clear back off the floor. The arena was ready.

MARY. And what happened then?

MOMMO. An' what happened then . . . Tired, tired.

MARY. Mommo?

MOMMO (*now regarding MARY with suspicion*). . . . . Shthap! . . . (*To herself.*) Tired . . . What's your business here? . . . There are no newses here for anyone about anything. Heh heh heh heh!

DOLLY. It's ten to ten. So he'll hardly come now, so off with yeh to sleep. There's the good girl, and we'll hear your confession again tomorrow night. There, there now. (*To MARY.*) That was a new bit. There, there now. She's in bye-byes.

MARY (*quietly*). She's not.

DOLLY. She's asleep! Mommo? . . . She's asleep, it's ten to ten. Ten to ten, 1984, and I read it – how long ago was it? – that by 1984 we'd all be going on our holidays to the moon in *Woman's Own*.

MARY. She's not asleep.

DOLLY. I'm not arg'in' about it. She's – resting.

MARY. And I'm going to rouse her again in a minute. You were saying?

DOLLY (*stretching herself, flaunting her stomach*). And a telly would fit nicely over there.

MARY. A plan, a proposition, you have it all figured out?

DOLLY. And I'm sorry now I spent the money on the video. No one uses it. You'd make more use of it. It has a remote. (*In answer to MARY's query 'remote'*.) Yeh know? One of them things yeh – (*hold in your hand*) –and – (*further demonstrates*) – control.

MARY. I have a video here already (*Mommo.*) What's your plan?

DOLLY. Wait'll we have a drink. She's guilty.

MARY. Guilty of what?

DOLLY. I don't know.

MARY. Then why –

DOLLY. I'm not arg'in' with yeh. (*Offering to top up MARY's drink.*)

MARY. Why can't you ever finish a subject or talk straight? I don't want another drink.

DOLLY. I'm talking straight.

MARY. What's on your mind, Dolly? I'm up to you.

DOLLY. There's no one up to Dolly.

MARY. Tck!

DOLLY. I'm talkin' straight!

Another car passes by outside.

Traffic. The weekend-long meeting at the computer plant place. And all the men, busy, locked outside the fence.

MARY (*abrupt movement to the table*). On second thoughts. (*And pours lemonade into her glass.*)

DOLLY (*is a bit drunk now and getting drunker*). No, wait a minute.

MARY. What-are-you-saying, Dolly?

DOLLY. An' that's why she goes on like a gramophone. Guilty.

MARY. This is nonsense.

DOLLY. And so are you.

MARY. So am I!

DOLLY. An' you owe me a debt.

MARY. What do I owe you?

DOLLY. *And* she *had* to get married.

MARY (*to herself*). Impossible.

DOLLY. No! No! – Mary? Wait a minute –

MARY (*fingers to her forehead*). Dolly, I'm –

DOLLY. I'm talkin' straight.

MARY. Trying to get a grip of – Ahmm. I'm trying to find – ahmm. Get control of – ahmm. My life, Dolly.

DOLLY. Yes. You're trying to say make head and tail of it all, talk straight, like myself. No, Mary, hold on! You told me one thing, I'll tell you another. D'yeh remember the pony-and-trap-Sunday-outings? I don't. But I remember – now try to contradict this – the day we buried Grandad. Now I was his favourite so I'll never forget it. And whereas – No, Mary! – whereas! She stood there over that hole in the ground like a rock – like a duck, like a duck, her chest stickin' out. Not a tear.

MARY. What good would tears have been?

DOLLY. Not a tear. And – *And!* – Tom buried in that same hole in the ground a couple of days before. Not a tear, then or since. (*Wandering to the table for another drink.*) Oh I gathered a few 'newses' about our Mommo.

MARY. Maybe she's crying now.

DOLLY. *All* of them had to get married except myself and Old Sharp Eyes. Mrs McGrath the sergeant said. But she bore a bastard all the same. Her Stephen. (*Wanders to the radio and switches it off.*) The hypocrite.

MARY. Leave it on.

DOLLY. I've a proposition.

MARY. It's the Sunday Concert. Switch it on.

DOLLY (*switches on the radio*). So what d'yeh think?

MARY. About what?

DOLLY. The slated (*gestures roof*), the other things I mentioned.

MARY. It would stop the place falling down for someone alright.

DOLLY. An' half of this place is mine, I'll sign it over.

MARY. To whom?

DOLLY. To whom. To Jack-Paddy-Andy, to Kitty-the-Hare, to you. And there might be – other things – you might need.

MARY. What else could anyone need?

DOLLY *now looking a bit hopeless, pathetic, offering a cigarette to* MARY, *lighting it for* MARY.

DOLLY. An' would you like another? (*drink*)

MARY *shakes her head.*

Lemonade?

MARY. No. What are you trying to say?

DOLLY. An' the turf out there won't last the winter.

MARY. You said that.

DOLLY. And one of the children.

She looks at MARY *for a reaction. But all this time* MARY's *mind, or half of it, is on* MOMMO.

Yeh. Company for yeh.

MARY. I get all this if I stay.

DOLLY. Or go.

MARY (*becoming more alert*). . . . What? . . . You want me to go? With one of the children? . . . *Which* one of the children?

DOLLY (*continues with closed eyes through the following*). Jesus, I'm tired. A brand new one.

MARY *laughs incredulously.*

Would you? Would you? Would you?

MARY. What?

DOLLY. Take him. It.

MARY. With me?

DOLLY (*nods*). An' no one need be any the wiser.

MARY. And if I stay?

DOLLY. Say it's yours. It'll all blow over in a month.

MARY. You're crazy.

DOLLY. That makes three of us. I'm not crazy. I'm – as you can see.

MARY. Yes. I've wondered for some time, but I thought you couldn't -- you couldn't! – be that stupid.

A car passes by outside.

DOLLY. More take-aways for the lads. (*She starts wearily for her coat.*) My, but they're busy.

MARY. No one is asking you to leave.

DOLLY (*stops. Eyes closed again*). You'll be paid.

MARY. I've heard you come up with a few things before, but!

DOLLY. Stephen'll kill me.

MARY. What about me?

DOLLY. Or he'll cripple me.

MARY. Do you ever think of others!

DOLLY. Or I'll fix him.

MARY. And you'll be out – gallivanting – again tomorrow night.

DOLLY. And the night after, and the night after. And you can be sure of that.

MARY. How long are you gone?

DOLLY. Six, seven months.

MARY. Six, seven months.

DOLLY. Trying to conceal it.

MARY. Who's the father?

DOLLY. I have my suspicions.

MARY. But he's busy perhaps tonight, picketing?

DOLLY. Yes, very busy. Travelling at the sound of speed. But the Chinese'll get them. (*Opens her eyes.*) Hmm?

MARY. And this is the help? This is what you've been figuring out?

DOLLY. You can return the child after, say, a year. If you want to.

MARY. I thought your figuring things out were about – ? (*She indicates* MOMMO. *Then she goes to* MOMMO.) Mommo, open your eyes, time to continue.

DOLLY. After a year it'll be easy to make up a story.

MARY. *Another* story! (*She laughs.*)

DOLLY. You're a nurse, you could help me if you wanted to.

MARY. Trying all my life to get out of *this* situation and now you want to present me with the muddle of your stupid life to make *sure* the saga goes on.

DOLLY. Oh the saga will go on.

MARY. Mommo!

DOLLY. I'll see to that, one way or the other.

MARY (*to herself*). I go away with a brand new baby. Mommo! (*To* DOLLY.) Where! Where do I go?

DOLLY *nods*.

You have that figured out too?

DOLLY. We can discuss that.

MARY *laughs*.

You're its aunt.

MARY. Its! (*She laughs*.)

DOLLY. Aunt! – Aunt! – And you're a nurse! – Aunt!

MARY. Mommo! I know you're not asleep.

DOLLY (*shrugs*). OK. (*Now talking to herself*.) And if it's a boy you can call it Tom, and if it's a girl you can call it Tom. (*Continues talking through the following, wandering to the fire and sitting there. DOLLY's speech, though to herself, dominating*.)

MOMMO. Supa milk, where's the milk?

MARY. Later.

MOMMO. Miss!

MARY. We're going to finish your nice story. Now! To continue. Where had you got to? Costello clearing his throat.

MOMMO. But in the jostlin' an' pushin' (*Eyes searching the floor*.) The sweets . . . the sweets . . .

DOLLY (*through the above*). But I've discussed something with someone. 'Cause if I don't get him he'll get me. But I know now how to get him and that's what got me saving, of late. I've made the preliminary enquiries. That little service of fixing someone is available — 'cause it's in demand — even round here. I've discussed it with someone.

MOMMO. The sweets.

MARY (*to DOLLY*). Have you finished?

DOLLY (*intensely*). You had it easy!

MARY. I had it easy? No one who came out of this — house — had it easy. (*To herself:*) I had it easy.

DOLLY. You-had-it-easy. The bright one, top of your class!

MARY (*to herself*). What would you know about it?

DOLLY. Top marks! — Hardly had your Leaving Cert, and you couldn't wait to be gone.

MARY. I won't deny that.

DOLLY. You can't! State Registered Nurse before you were twenty —

MARY. Twenty-one —

DOLLY. A Sister before you were twenty-five, Assistant Matron at the age of thirty.

MARY. And a midwife.

DOLLY. Yes, SRN, CMB, DDT!

MARY. All very easy.

DOLLY. Couldn't get away fast enough.

MARY. But I came back, Dolly.

DOLLY. Aren't you great?

MARY. I failed. It all failed. I'm as big a failure as you, and that's some failure.

DOLLY *is stopped for a moment by* MARY's *admission.*

You hadn't considered that?

MOMMO *has started rambling again, repeating the last section of the story which she told earlier, down to 'The arena was ready'.*

MOMMO. An' sure they could have got home. An' the small stranger, her husband sure, was goin' out to check the weather, for as had been forecasted the thaw was . . .

DOLLY (*her voice over* MOMMO's). No! No! You had it easy! – You had it – You had – I had – I had ten! – I had a lifetime! – A lifetime! – Here with herself, doin' her every bidding, listenin' to her seafóid (*rambling*) gettin' worse till I didn't know where I was! – Pissin' in the bed beside me – I had a lifetime! Then the great Stephen – the surprise of it! comes coortin'! Never once felt any – real – warmth from him – what's wrong with him? – but he's my rescuer, my saviour. But then, no rhyme or reason to it – He could've got a job at that plant, but he couldn't wait to be gone either! Then waitin' for the hero, my rescuer, the sun shining out of his eighty-five-pounds-a-week arse, to come home at Christmas. No interest in me – oh, he used me! – or in children, or the rotten thatch or the broken window, or Conor above moving in his fence from *this* side. I'm fightin' all the battles. Still fightin' the battles. And what d'yeh think he's doin' now this minute? Sittin' by the hearth in Coventry, is he? Last Christmas an' he was hardly off the bus, Old Sharp Eyes whisperin' into his ear about me. Oooo, but he waited. Jesus, how I hate him! Jesus, how I hate them! Men! Had his fun and games with me that night, *and* first thing in the morning. Even sat down to eat the hearty breakfast I made. Me thinkin', still no warmth, but maybe it's goin' to be okay. Oooo, but I should've known from *experience* about-the-great-up-stand-in'-Steph-en-evrabody's-fav-our-ite.

Because, next thing he has me by the hair of the head, fistin'
me down in the mouth. Old Sharp Eyes there, noddin' her
head every time he struck an' struck an' kicked an' kicked an'
pulled me round the house by the hair of the head. Jesus,
men! (*Indicating the outdoors where she had her sex.*) You-
think-I-enjoy? I-use-*them*! Jesus, hypocrisy! An' then, me left
with my face like a balloon – you saw a lot of me last
Christmas' didn't yeh? – my body black and blue, the street
angel an' his religious mother – 'As true as Our Lady is in
heaven now, darlin's' – over the road to visit you an'
Mommo with a little present an' a happy an' a holy
Christmas now darlin's an' blessed St-fuckin'-Jude an' all the
rest of them flyin' about for themselves up there.

MOMMO. The arena was ready. A laughing competition there
would be. (*She coughs in preparation.*)

DOLLY (*at* MOMMO). Och hona ho gus hah-haa! Jesus, how
I hate them! I hate her (*Mommo*) – I hate this house – She
hates you – I hate my own new liquorice-all-sorts-coloured
house –

MARY, DOLLY *speaking simultaneously.*

MARY (*ashen-face, shaking her head*). No . . . No.

DOLLY. She! – She! – She hates you!

MARY. No.

MOMMO, DOLLY *speaking simultaneously.*

MOMMO. 'Wuff a wuff!' A wuha wuha wuha wuha, wock-ock
och ock och och ock – Naaw.'

DOLLY. And I hate you!

MARY. Why?

DOLLY. Why!

MOMMO. 'Heh heh heh heh,' proud, aisy an' gentle.

DOLLY. You don't know terror, you don't know hatred, you don't know desperation!

MOMMO. An' sure Costello's laughin' wasn't right at all.

DOLLY. No one came out of this house had it easy but you had it easy.

MOMMO. 'Quock uck-uck-uck-uck quock?' (MOMMO *unwrapping a sweet and putting it in her mouth.*)

MARY. Dolly, stop it at once!

DOLLY. 'Dolly, stop it at once.' Look, go away an' stay away.

MARY. Dolly!

MOMMO. 'Heh heh heh heh heh.'

DOLLY. 'This is our home' – You'll need a few bob. I'll give it to you, and my grand plan: I'll look after things here, all fronts, including lovee lovee Mommo, an' Stephen'll never raise a finger to me again.

MARY. You're –

DOLLY. Am I?

MARY. You're –

DOLLY. Am I? We'll see – Hah! – if I'm bluffing.

MARY. Have you finished ranting?

DOLLY. Ooh, ranting!

MOMMO (*looking at the floor*). The sweets . . . the sweets (*Whispering.*)

MARY. You're spoilt, you're unhappy, you're running round in circles.

DOLLY. *I'm* running round in circles? Suitcase packed – How many times? Puttin' on airs – look at the boots, look at the lady! You're stayin', you're goin', 'I need to talk to someone'

– Fuck off! 'I wanted to come home, I had to come home' –
Fuck off!

MARY. Stop it this moment, I won't have it! You're frightening
her.

*In reply to 'frightening her', DOLLY indicates MOMMO
who is now sucking a sweet, lost in her own thoughts. Then
DOLLY turns to look into the fire, her back to MARY; she
continues in quieter tone.*

DOLLY. The countryside produced a few sensations in the last
couple of years, but my grand plan: I'll show them what can
happen in the dark of night in a field. I'll come to grips with
my life.

Short silence.
MOMMO's eyes fixed on MARY.

MOMMO. Miss? . . . Do I know you?

*MARY shakes her head, 'No'; she is afraid to speak; if she
does she will cry.*

. . . Pardon?

MARY shakes her head.

DOLLY (*to the fire*). I'll finish another part of this family's
history in grander style than any of the others.

MARY. . . . The arena was ready.

MOMMO. 'Twas.

MARY. But Costello's laugh wasn't right at all.

MOMMO. Then ''Scuse me a minute,' says he lickin' his big
mouth, puts a spit in the one hand, then one in the other, an'
ponderin' the third that he sent to the floor. (*Coughs.*) 'A
wuff.'

DOLLY. A wuff, wuff!

MOMMO. 'A wuha wuha wuha wuha, a wuha huha huha hoo,
quock-uckina na hoona ho ho, a wo ho ho ho ho ho ho!' An'
twasn't bad at all. Was it? An' Costello knew it. An' by way

of exper'ment, though 'twasn't his turn, had a go at it again, his ear cocked to himself.

DOLLY. Heh heh heh heh heh heh heh heh – We filled half that graveyard.

MOMMO. We did. But then, ''Scuse me too,' says the stranger makin' Costello, stiffen, an' 'Heh heh heh, heh heh heh, heh heh heh,' chuckled he.

DOLLY. Heh heh heh, heh heh heh, heh heh heh heh – Well, I'll fill the other half.

MARY (*ferociously at* DOLLY). Shthap!

DOLLY. Och hona ho gus hah-haa!

MOMMO. Pardon?

MARY (*to* MOMMO). . . . No, you don't know me. But I was here once, and I ran away to try and blot out here. I didn't have it easy. Then I tried bad things, for a time, with someone. So I came back, thinking I'd find – something – here, or, if I didn't, I'd put everything right, Mommo? And tonight I thought I'd make a last try. Live out the – story – finish it, move on to a place where, perhaps, we could make some kind of new start. I want to help you.

DOLLY. And yourself.

MARY. And myself. Mommo?

MOMMO. Where's the milk for the night?

MARY *nods that she will get it.*

MOMMO. Tck!

MARY (*gently to* DOLLY). She may hate me, you may hate me. But I don't hate her. I love her for what she's been through, and she's all that I have. So she has to be my only consideration. She doesn't understand. Do you understand, Dolly? Please . . . And I'm sorry.

DOLLY (*drunkenly*). For what?

MARY (*turns away tearfully*). I'm not the saint you think I am.

DOLLY. The what? Saint? That'd be an awful thing to be. 'Wo ho ho, ho ho ho!'

MARY *puts the milk by the bed.*

MOMMO. Yis. Did yeh hear? The full style *was* returnin' – 'Wo ho ho, wo ho ho!' An' like a great archbishop turnin' on his axis, nods an' winks to his minions that he knew all along. The cheers that went up in John Mah'ny's that night!

An' now what did they start doin', the two gladiators, circlin' the floor, eyes riveted together, silent in quietude to find the advantage, save the odd whoop from Costello, his fist through the ceilin', an' the small little stranger'd bate the odd little dance.

Now. Then. And.

'Yeh sold all your cargo?' Costello roarin' it like a master to friken a scholar. The laugh from his attendants, but then so did the stranger.

'Where (*are*) yeh bound for?' – stern Costello – 'Your destination, a Mhico?'

'Ballindineside, your worship.'

'Ballindineside, a Thighearna!'

DOLLY. Oh ho ho, wo ho ho.

MOMMO. 'Cunn ether iss syha soory.' (*Coinn iotair is saidhthe suaraighe*)

DOLLY. Hounds of rage and bitches of wickedness!

MOMMO. An' the description despicable more fitting their own place.

DOLLY (*to the fire, almost dreamily*). Why the fuck did he marry me?

It only lasts a second, but MARY *holds a glance on the now pathetic-looking* DOLLY.

MOMMO. 'A farmer?' says Costello. 'A goose one,' says the stranger. An' t'be fair to the Bochtáns they plauded the self-denigration.

DOLLY. I don't hate anyone.

MOMMO. 'An' yourself?' says the stranger. 'Oh now you're questionin' me,' says Costello, 'An' Rabbits,' screeches Josie, 'Hull-hull-hull, hull-hull-hull!'

DOLLY (*stands*). What did I get up for?

    MARY and DOLLY forget themselves and start laughing at MOMMO's dramatisation of this section.

MOMMO. An' Rabbits!' says the stranger. 'Rabbits!' says he, 'heh-heh.' 'Well, heh heh heh, heh heh heh, heh heh heh, heh heh heh!' 'What's the cause of your laughter?' Costello frownin' moroya. (*Mar dhea; pretending seriousness*) 'Bunny rabbits! says the stranger – is *that* what you're in!'

    MARY and DOLLY laughing their own laughter.

    'Not at all, me little man,' says Costello, 'I've a herd of trinamanooses in Closh back the road.'
      'Tame ones?' says the stranger.
      'Tame ones, what else, of a certainty,' says Costello, 'An' the finest breed for 'atin' sure!'
      'But for the Townies though for 'atin',' says the stranger, most sincerely. An' not able to keep the straight face, Costello roared out a laughter, an' gave beck to his attendants to plaud the stranger's cleverality.

    The three of them laughing.

    Now wasn't he able for them?

DOLLY. Where's the flashlamp?

MOMMO. An' the contrariety an' venom was in it while ago!

DOLLY. I want to go out the back.

MARY. It's on top of the dresser.

MOMMO. But now they couldn't do enough for that decent man an' woman, all vying with each other – an' sure they didn't have it – to buy treats for the strangers, tumblers of whiskey an' bumpers of port wine. A strange auld world right enough. But in some wisdom of his own he made it this way. 'Twas the nicest night ever.

DOLLY (*has got the flashlamp; a plea in her voice*). Mary?

MARY. 'Twas the nicest night ever.

MOMMO. But they'd yet to find the topic would keep them laughin' near forever.

DOLLY. Mary?

MARY. Topic?

MOMMO. Then one'd laugh solo, the other'd return, then Costello'd go winkin' an' they'd both laugh together, a nod from the stranger (*and*) they'd stop that same moment to urge riotous chorus, give the others a chance.

DOLLY. Don't want the fuggin' flashlamp. (*She discards it. Then, as if driving cattle out of the house, she goes out the back door.*) How! – How! – How! Hup! – Skelong! – Bleddy cows! Howa-that-how! – Hup! Hup!

MARY. What topic did they find?

MOMMO. But there can be no gainsayin' it, Costello clear had the quality laugh. 'Wo ho ho, ho ho ho', (in) the barrel of his chest would great rumbles start risin', the rich rolls of round sound out of his mouth, to explode in the air an' echo back rev'berations. The next time demonstratin' the range of his skill, go flyin' aloft (to) the heights of registration – 'Hickle-ickle-ickle-ickle!' – like a hen runnin' demented from the ardent attentions, over-persistent, of a cock in the yard after his business. Now!

MARY. What about Grandad?

MOMMO. Who?

MARY. The stranger.

MOMMO. Not much by way of big sound?

MARY. No.

MOMMO. Or rebounding modulation?

MARY. No.

MOMMO. But was that a stipulation?

MARY. No.

MOMMO. He knew the tricks of providence and was cunning of exertion. Scorn for his style betimes?

MARY *nods*.

But them wor his tactics.

MARY. And he was the one most in control.

MOMMO. He was. (*She yawns.*) Tired.

MARY. No, Mommo. It *is* a nice story. And you've nearly told it all tonight. Except for the last piece that you never tell. Hmm?

MOMMO. Who was that woman?

MARY. What woman?

MOMMO. Tck! – That woman just went out the door there. (*Mimicking* DOLLY.) 'Hup-hup-howa that'?

MARY. That was Dolly . . . Dolly.

MOMMO. An' does she always behave that way?

MARY. Sometimes.

MOMMO (*thinking about this; it does not make sense to her. Then eyes scrutinising* MARY: *in this moment she is possibly close to recognising* MARY). . . . Who are (*you*)?

MARY. Try a guess. Yes, Mommo? – Yes, Mommo? – Please – who am I?

MOMMO. Here she is again!

DOLLY *comes in. She looks bloated and tired. She wolfs down the slice of cake which she deliberately resisted earlier. Then looking for her bag, putting on her overcoat, etc.*

DOLLY. And I've been starving myself.

MOMMO (*whispering*). She'd eat yeh out of house an' home . . . Is there something you require, Miss, that you're rummaging for over there?

DOLLY (*realises she is being spoken to*). Your pension.

MOMMO. Oh it's time for ye both to be going – ten to ten. He doesn't like calling when there's strangers in the house.

MARY. We're off now in a minute. What was that topic again that kept them on laughing?

MOMMO. Misfortunes. (*She yawns.*)

MARY. Mommo? (MOMMO's *eyes are closed.*)

DOLLY (*to herself, looking at the door*). I hate going home.

MARY. Mommo? Or if you like, the bit about 'Out of the bushes more of them was comin'.'

MOMMO. Tom is in Galway. (*Opens her eyes.*) I bet him with nettles. Mitchin' from school. D'yeh think he remembers?

MARY (*gently*). No.

MOMMO (*closes her eyes*). Well, I don't remember . . . I don't remember any more of it.

MARY (*tired, futile*). And out of the bushes more of them was comin'?

MOMMO (*drowsily*). I don't remember any more of it.

MARY. Wherever their hovels were, holes in the ground . . . 'cause 'twas place of desolation.

DOLLY (*another plea*). Mary?

MARY (*eyes continue on* MOMMO *who is now asleep*). Sit down.

DOLLY *remains standing, wondering is there hope for her in* MARY's *remark.*

DOLLY. . . . What were you trying to do with her?

MARY. 'Twas only a notion . . . She's asleep.

DOLLY. . . . Maybe she'd wake up again?

MARY (*slight shake of her head, 'No'*). Sit down.

DOLLY (*sits*). . . . What're yeh goin' to do?

MARY (*slight shake of her head, a tremulous sigh*). Ahmm.

DOLLY. . . . Back to the nursing?

Slight shake of the head from MARY.

. . . What?

MARY. No. That wasn't me at all. And no confidence now anyway. (*She collects up a few odds and ends and puts them in the suitcase.*) Who's looking after the children?

DOLLY. Maisie Kelly. They're stayin' the night in her house. She knows. She said if I had to go away for a day or anything . . . I don't want to go away.

MARY (*absently*). The nicest night ever.

DOLLY. . . . What were we doin' that night?

MARY. Ahmm. The shade on that light: do you mind if I? (*She switches off the light and lights a candle.*) We let the fire go out. The cursèd paraffin.

MARY *has collected up a silver-backed hairbrush and a clothes brush.*

DOLLY. . . . But if you're not going back to the nursing?

MARY. There must be *something*, some future for me, somewhere. (*She is brushing the back of* DOLLY's *coat*.) I can certainly scrub floors.

DOLLY (*a little irritably*). What're you doin'?

MARY. Just a little – dust – here.

DOLLY. Who cares?

MARY. It's just that people talk at the slightest.

DOLLY. Na bac na ciaróigí (*ciaróga*). (*Don't mind the gossipers*)

MARY. When I was a nurse there was a patient, terminal, an elderly woman and we became very close.

DOLLY. Do you care what people say?

MARY. I'm afraid I do. There. (*The coat is brushed; she now brushes* DOLLY's *hair*.) I don't know why she used to watch me or why she chose to make friends with me.

DOLLY. What are you doin' now?

MARY. But one day she said, in the middle of – whatever – conversation we were having. 'You're going to be alright, Mary.' Simple remark. But it took me by surprise. Like, a *promised* blessing. And why I should have – (*Shrugs.*) believed in it for, oh, twenty years? until recently, I don't know. There. (DOLLY's *hair is brushed.*) She left me these (*the brushes*) and this (*the teapot*) and the book. (*She dumps the lot into the suitcase.*)

DOLLY. If I sat down to write a book.

MARY. Though the book has always depressed me a bit. *Winter Words*. I can't do a thing for you, Dolly. Can you lend me a hundred quid?

DOLLY *nods*.

Well, that's it then.

DOLLY *is just sitting there looking into the fire;* MARY *standing, her back to the suitcase, her hands resting on it: two figures frozen in time. Then the cortège of cars approaching, passing the house (at comparatively slow speed).*

DOLLY. The funeral. The weekend-long meeting is over. Now are they travelling at the sound of speed?

MARY *laughs.*

I told you the Chinese'd get them.
(*They are beginning to laugh. Looking at her stomach — the bulge.*) Good man Josie!

MARY *laughs.* DOLLY *joins in the laughter,* DOLLY *flaunting herself, clowning.*

And you're his aunt!

They laugh louder, the laughter getting out of hand.

(*To her stomach*). Good man Josie! . . . (*Uproariously.*) Jesus, misfortunes!

Then the unexpected, MOMMO's *voice.*

MOMMO. What time is it?

Silence.

MARY. Seven. (*In a whisper, waiting, frozen.*)

MOMMO. Explosions of laughter an' shouts of hurrahs!

DOLLY (*sits heavily on the bed*). Jesus, I'm tired.

MARY (*pleading with* DOLLY). Dolly!

MOMMO. For excess of joy.

DOLLY. 'S alright, 'salright, Mommo: I'm Dolly, I'm like a film star. (*To* MARY.) 'S alright.

MOMMO. An' didn't he ferret out her eyes to see how she was farin', an' wasn't she titherin' with the best of them an' weltin' her thighs. No heed on her now to be gettin' on home.

No. But offerin' to herself her own congratulations at hearin'
herself laughin'. An' then, like a girl, smiled at her husband,
an' his smile back so shy, like the boy he was in youth. An'
the moment was for them alone. Unawares of all cares,
unawares of all the others. An' how long before since their
eyes had met, mar gheal dhá gréine, glistenin' for each other.
Not since long and long ago.

    And now Costello's big hand was up for to call a recession.
'But how,' says he, 'is it to be indisputably decided who is the
winner?' And a great silence followed. None was forgettin'
this was a contest. An' the eyes that wor dancin', now
pending the answer, glazed an' grave in dilation: 'Twas a
difficult question. (*Quietly.*) Och-caw. Tired of waiting male
intelligence. 'He who laughs last' says she.

    An' 'cause 'twas a woman that spoke it, I think Costello
was frikened, darts class of a glance at her an' – (*She gulps.*)
'That's what I thought,' says he.

    But wasn't that his mistake? ever callin' the recession an' he
in full flight. 'Cause now, ready himself as he would, with his
coughin' an' spittin', the sound emanating from a man of his
talent, so forced and ungracious, he'd stop it himself.

    (*Whispering.*) 'He's lost it,' says someone (Her derisory
shout on the night.) Och hona ho gus hah-haa! (*Whispering.*)
'He should never have stopped.' Their faces like mice.

    An' he'd tempt it an' 'tempt it an' 'tempt it again. Ach an
fear mór as Bochtán (*But the big man from Bochtán*) in
respiratory disaster is i ngreas casachtaí (*and in bouts of
coughing*). (*She coughs . . .*) The contest was over.

MARY. The contest was over?

MOMMO. 'Twas.

MARY. The contest was over?

MOMMO. The contest was over. Oh the strangers'd won.

MARY. But what about the topic?

MOMMO. Hah?

MARY. Would keep them laughing near forever.

MOMMO (*whispers*). Misfortunes . . . *She* supplied them with
   the topic. And it started up again with the subject of potatoes,
   the damnedable crop was in that year.
      'Wet an' wat'rey?' says the stranger.
      'Wet an' wat'rey,' laughing Costello.
      'Heh heh heh, but not blighted?'
      'No ho ho, ho ho ho, but scabby an' small.'
      'Sour an' soapy – Heh heh heh.'
      'Yis – ho ho ho,' says the hero. 'Hard to wash, ladies?
   Hard to boil, ladies?'
      'An' the divil t'ate – Heh heh heh!'
      But they were only getting into their stride.
      'An' the hay?' says old Brian, 'behell.'
      'Rotted!' says the contestants, roarin' it together.
      'The bita oats,' shouts young Kemple – 'Jasus!' Lodged in
   the field. An' the turf says another. Still in the bog, laughed
   the answer. An' the chickens the pip, pipes up the old crone.
   An' the sheep, the staggers, an' the cow that just died, an' the
   man that was in it lost both arms to the thresher. An' the
   dead!

MARY. . . . And the dead, Mommo?

MOMMO (*whimpers*). I wanta see mah father.

MARY. Who were the dead?

MOMMO. Pardon? Skitherin' an' laughin' – Hih-hih-hih – at
   their nearest an' dearest. Her Pat was her eldest, died of
   consumption, had his pick of the girls an' married the widdy
   again' all her wishes. The decline in that fambly, she knew the
   widdy'd outlast him. She told them the story – Hih-hih-hih –
   an' many another. An' how Pat, when he came back for the
   two sheep (*that*) wor his – An' they wor – An' he was her
   first-born. But you'll not have them she told him. Soft Willie
   inside, quiet by the hearth, but she knew he'd be able, the
   spawgs of hands he had on him. 'Is it goin' fightin' me own
   brother?' But she told him a brother was one thing, but she
   was his mother, an' them were the orders to give Pat the high
   road, and no sheep, one, two or three wor leavin' the yard.

They hurted each other. An' how Pat went back empty to his
strap of a widdy, an' was dead within a six months. Hih-hih-
hih. (*The 'hih-hih-hih' which punctuate her story sounds
more like tears – ingrown sobs – rather than laughter.*) Oh
she made great contributions, rollcalling the dead. Was she
what or 'toxicated? An' for the sake of an auld ewe was stuck
in the flood was how she lost two of the others, Jimmy and
Michael. Great gales of laughter to follow each name of the
departed. Hih-hih-hih. An' the nice wife was near her time,
which one of them left behind him?

MARY. Daddy.

MOMMO. Died tryin' to give birth to the fourth was to be in
it. An' she herself left with the care of three small childre
waitin'. All contributions receiving volleys of cheers. Nothin'
was sacred an' nothing a secret. The unbaptised an' stillborn
in shoeboxes planted, at the dead hour of night treading
softly the Lisheen to make the regulation hole – not more, not
less than two feet deep – too fearful of the field, haunted by
infants, to speak or to pray. They were fearful of their ankles
– Hih-hih-hih. An' tryin' not to hasten, steal away again,
leaving their pagan parcels in isolation forever. Hih-hih-hih.
Her soft Willie was her pet went foreign after the others. An'
did she drive them all away? Never ever to be heard of, ever
again: Save soft Willie, aged thirty-four, in Louisaville
Kentucky, died, peritonites. Spell that. A-N-T Yes? I-P-H.
Yes? F-U-L- Yes? L-O-G- Yes? E-S-T- Yes? I-N-E-
Antiphfullogestine, Now! That's how I taught them all to
spell. Hih-hih-hih! The nicest night they ever had, that's what
I'm sayin'. The stories kept on comin' an' the volleys and
cheers. All of them present, their heads threwn back
abandoned in festivities of guffaws: the wretched and
neglected, dilapidated an' forlorn, the forgotten an'
tormented, the lonely an' despairing, ragged an' dirty,
impoverished, hungry, emaciated and unhealthy, eyes big as
saucers, ridiculing an' defying of their lot on earth below –
glintin' their defiance – their defiance an' rejection, inviting of
what else might come or *care* to come! – driving bellows of

refusal at the sky through the roof. Och hona ho gus hah-
haa! . . . The nicest night ever.

MARY. An' what else was to come?

MOMMO. Nothing.

MARY. Tom.

MOMMO. Tom is in Galway.

MARY. Grandad.

MOMMO. An' when I told me father what did he say? "Twas
a *double* insolence at heaven.' We weren't meant to be here at
all! 'Making mock of God's prize piece, its structure and
system.' 'Oh,' he groaned. 'I have wrestled with enigmals (*all*)
my life-long years. I've combed all of creation,' that man
intoned, 'and in the wondrous handiwork of God, have found
only two flaws, man an' the earwig. Of what use is man,
what utility the earwig, where do they either fit in the system?
They are both specimens desperate, without any control, and
therefore unfree. One cocks his head,' says he, 'the other his
tail. But God will not be mocked. Especially when He was so
clever at creating all things else. Still, God must have said, I'll
leave them there an' see what transpires.' An' says me father
– (*She winks shrewdly.*) 'Maybe the earwig isn't doin' too
bad at all.' An' then he tied his hands.

MARY. Who did?

MOMMO. Tck! Me father. That 'twas a double insolence at
heaven. But they'd soon get their answer.

MARY. Who would?

MOMMO. The Bochtáns, the Bochtáns sure! Tck! Mauleogs
drunk?

MARY *nods.*

Them all packed together?

MARY *nods.*

The foul odour that was in it, you'd hardly get your breath. The ache was in the laughter. The two contestants sweating, the big man most profusely. Sure they'd been contending the title now for five or six hours. An' Costello, openin' down his shirts an' loosenin' his buckle, was doublin' up an' staggerin' an' holdin' his sides. 'Aw Jasus, lads, ye have me killed – Hickle-ickle-ickle,' an' the laughing lines upon his mien wor more like lines of pain. An' the stranger goin' 'Heh heh heh heh, heh heh heh heh,' aisy an' gentle. Then beholding his 'ponent from contortion to convulsion, his complexion changin' colours an' arrivin' at purple: 'Heh heh heh heh, heh heh . . . heh . . . heh . . . heh,' the frown to his brow bringin' stillness upon him an' the two little smiles to the sides of his mouth. Suddenly he shouts, 'Costello's the winner!' But sure they wouldn't have it – nor herself in the corner. 'He's nat (*not*), he's nat, he's nat, he's nat!' 'On, on-on, Bochtán forever!'

'No-no! – Heh-heh – he has me bet!'

'He's nat, he's nat, he's nat, he's nat!'

The others, 'Up Bochtán – On Bochtán! Bochtán forever!'

An' Costello now all the while in upper registration – 'Hickle-ickle-ickle-ickle' – longin' to put stop to it, his own cacklin' wouldn't let him. An' 'deed, when he'd tempt to rise an arm – an' sure he wasn't able – in gesture of cessation, th' other mistakin' of his purpose would go thinkin' t' do it for'm (*for him*) puncturin' holes in the ceilin', batin' stomps on the floor.

An' the stranger now could only stand and watch. An' late it was herself realised the Great Adversary had entered.

'Hickle-ickle-ickle-ickle – Aw Jasus, lads, I'm dyin', – Oh not without effort. Hickle, ickle, ickle, ickle. Then slow in a swoon he went down to the floor. For the last moments were left him 'twas the stranger that held him, for there was nothing in the world to save him, or able to save him. Now!

MARY. And what's the rest of it?

MOMMO. Pardon?

MARY. For there was nothing now in the world? Only a little bit left.

MOMMO (*musing*). For there was nothing now in the world . . .

DOLLY *is stirring in her sleep and wakes up for a moment.*

DOLLY. Mary?

MARY (*regards her gravely for a moment; then*). . . . You're going to be alright, Dolly. Roll in under the blanket.

DOLLY *goes back to sleep.*

MOMMO. To save him . . . Or able to save him. Did I not say that? Oh yis. 'An' the rabbits, lads,' says Cost'llo, 'I didn't sell e'er the one of them, but threwn them comin' home for fun again' Patch Curran's door.' And that was the last he was to utter that night or any other.

MARY. They don't laugh there anymore.

MOMMO. Save the childre, until they arrive at the age of reason. Now! Bochtán forever is Bailegangaire.

Through the following MARY *undresses behind the headboard and puts on her long simple nightdress; she lets down her hair, gets the hairbrush from the case and brushes her hair. Switches off the radio. She looks remarkably beautiful; she is like a young elegant woman, her face introspective and grave.*

MARY. To conclude.

MOMMO. To conclude. The thaw as was forecasted was in it, an' the strangers went home.

MARY. But didn't they hurt grandad? . . . The stranger, his ribs?

MOMMO. They did. But he bet them – he bet the best of them.

MARY. And wasn't his face cut?

MOMMO. Oh they did. They did. They wor for lettin' them
home. D'yeh know? Home without hinder. Till the thief,
Josie, started cryin', cryin' at death, and was insistently
demanding the boots be took of the stranger to affirm 'twas
feet or no was in them. An' from trying to quieten his
gathering excitement someone of them got hit. Then he struck
back. Till they forgot what they wor doin' sure, or how it had
started, but all drawin' kicks an' blows, one upon the other,
till the venom went rampant. They pulled him down off the
cart an' gave him the kickin'. They did. Oh they gave him
such a doin', till John Mah'ny an' the curate (*that*) was called
prevailed again' the Bolsheviks.

MARY *gets into bed beside* MOMMO.
DOLLY *is asleep on the other side.*

'Twas dawn when they got home. Not without trepidation?
But the three small childre, like ye, their care, wor safe an'
sound fast asleep on the settle. Now, my fondlings, settle
down an' be sayin' yere prayers. I forget what happened the
three sticks of rock. Hail Holy Queen. Yes? Mother of
Mercy. Yes? Hail our lives? Yes? Our sweetness and our
hope.

MARY. It was a bad year for the crops, a good one for
mushrooms, and the three small children were waiting for
their gran and their grandad to come home. Mommo? My
bit. Mary was the eldest. She was the clever one, and she was
seven. Dolly, the second, was like a film-star and she was
grandad's favourite. And they were in and out of the road
watching for the horse and cart. Waiting for ribbons. And
Tom who was the youngest, when he got excited would go
pacing o'er and o'er the boundary of the yard. He had
confided in Mary his expectation. They would be bringing
him his dearest wish – grandad told him secretly – a mouth
organ for Christmas. That was alright. But in the – excitement
– of their waiting they forgot to pay attention to the fire.
Then Mary and Dolly heard – 'twas like an explosion. Tom
had got the paraffin and, not the way grandad did it, stholled

it on to the embers, and the sudden blaze came out on top of him. And when they ran in and . . . saw him, Mary got . . . hysterical. And Dolly following suit got the same. Then Mary sent Dolly across the fields for May Glynn. And sure May was only . . . eleven? Then Mary covered . . . the wounds . . . from the bag of flour in the corner. She'd be better now, and quicker now, at knowing what to do. And then May Glynn's mother came and they took Tom away to Galway, where he died . . . Two mornings later, and he had only just put the kettle on the hook, didn't grandad, the stranger, go down too, slow in a swoon . . . Mommo?

MOMMO. It got him at last.

MARY. Will you take your pills now?

MOMMO. The yellow ones.

MARY. Yes.

MOMMO. Poor Séamus.

MOMMO *takes the pills with a sup of milk.* (*Perhaps it is now that* MARY *gets into the bed.*)

MARY. Is there anything else you need?

MOMMO. To thee do we cry. Yes? Poor banished children of Eve.

MARY. Is there anything you have to say to me?

MOMMO. Be sayin' yere prayers now an' ye'll be goin' to sleep. To thee do we send up our sighs. Yes? For yere Mammy an' Daddy an' grandad is (*who are*) in heaven.

MARY. And Tom.

MOMMO. Yes. An' he only a ladeen was afeared of the gander. An' tell them ye're all good. Mourning and weeping in this valley of tears. (*She is handing the cup back to* MARY.) And sure a tear isn't such a bad thing, Mary, and haven't we everything we need here, the two of us. (*And she settles down to sleep.*)

MARY (*tears of gratitude brim to her eyes; fervently*). Oh we have, Mommo.

Her tears continue to the end but her crying is infused with a sound like the laughter of relief.

. . . To conclude. It's a strange old place, alright, in whatever wisdom He has to have made it this way. But in whatever wisdom there is, in the year 1984, it was decided to give that – fambly . . . of strangers another chance, and a brand new baby to gladden their home.

Schubert's 'Notturno' comes in under Mary's final speech. The lights fade.

A Thief of a Christmas

The Actuality of how Bailegangaire came by its appellation

A Thief of a Christmas was first produced at The Abbey Theatre, Dublin in December 1985, with the following cast:

JOHN	Peadar Lamb
JOHN'S WIFE	Bríd Ní Neachtain
BINA	May Cluskey
STEPHEN	Mícheál Ó Briain
JOSIE	Garrett Keogh
MARTIN JOHN	Macdara O Fatharta
BRIAN	Paul Bennett
ANTHONY	Darragh Kelly
TOMÁS RUA	Dónall Farmer
PEGGY	Eithne Dempsey
STRANGER	Bob Carlile
STRANGER'S WIFE	Joan O'Hara
COSTELLO	Mick Lally

Community: Niall O'Brien, Joy Forsythe, Eleanor Feely, Sarah Carroll, Michelle O'Connor, Anne Enright, Marie Sutton, Joan Fogarty, Helen Nugent, Deirdre Herbert, David Herlihy, Niall O'Keefe, Patrick Brady, Paud Murray, Conday Conarain, Michael O'Doherty, Ray Cooke, Noel O'Donovan, Bill Cowley, Lorraine Bond.

Children: Nell Murphy, Eoin Sharp, Elaine Grace, Martin Lynch, Jane O'Reilly.

Musicians: Mícheál Mac Aogáin, Mícheál O Briain, Antoin Mac Gabhann.

Director Roy Heayberd
Settings & Costumes Chisato Yoshimi
Lighting Tony Wakefield
Musical Director Mícheál Mac Aogáin
Fight Director Mark Shelley

Place: A pub-cum-general store in a remote village
Time: About 50 years ago

Characters

JOHN'S WIFE
BINA
STEPHEN
BRIAN
JOSIE
COSTELLO
JOHN
MARTIN JOHN
ANTHONY
TOMÁS RUA
STRANGER
STRANGER'S WIFE

Others: Peggy and other villagers; a fiddler and a melodeon player (the musicians can be male or female, or one of each sex).

ACT ONE

Christmas is a matter of days away. It is about six o'clock and darkness has fallen. Oil lamps light the pub-cum-general stores. Groceries, sweets, items of clothing and hardware, JOHN'S cubby-hole of an office (which is also, probably, the Post Office) at the end nearest the front door. At the other end of the rough counter is the pub. Here we have an open fire, timber forms and timber 'half' barrels provide the seating; a low ceiling. A door behind the counter leads to the kitchen and living quarters. All quite primitive. We are dealing with a neglected, forgotten peasantry.

Two old men, BRIAN and STEPHEN are seated by the fire, pints beside them. A FIDDLER in a corner is putting resin on his bow. But it is on JOHN'S WIFE, a young buxom woman in her twenties, that the lights come up. She is attending a customer at the shop end, entering items in a ledger.

JOHN'S WIFE. Six tallow Christmas candles for to put in your windows, a pair of black laces for your Sunday boots, a fine-tooth comb, a half-a-pound of black puddin'. (*She stoops to pick up an INFANT who has started to whinge, hidden behind the counter.*) And what else was there?

The customer she is attending to is BINA, a crone, dressed in a mixture of traditional clothing and the gaudy cast-offs of a girl. A bandage over one eye.

BINA. The laxatives.

JOHN'S WIFE. He's going to kill himself eating them laxatives.

BINA. Sure none can stop him, he thinks they're sweets and will have nothing else.

JOHN'S WIFE. You're too good to him. Now: tobaccy, iceing sugar, raisins, Bex tartar – Isn't it very quiet, Bina? – matches.

BINA. And the salt, ma'am.

JOHN'S WIFE. Them all away at the Big Market. (*Writing.*) S.A.L.T. But the roads are bad for them getting home. And was there anything else you required?

BINA. The usual drop of –

She leaves it unfinished, another musician is entering – an ACCORDIANIST (*can be a man or a woman*).

JOHN'S WIFE. Aw! you're back again for us this year, Kate/ Willie.

ACCORDIANIST. And I had the time of it getting here. How are ye all?

JOHN'S WIFE. Grand! McDonagh (*the fiddler*) is waitin' ablow (*below*) for yeh.

The ACCORDIANIST *joins the* FIDDLER.

We'll have the night of it.

BINA. We will as always. And the singing!

JOHN'S WIFE. And the dancing! An' what were yeh saying?

BINA. The naggin of brandy.

JOHN'S WIFE (*conspiratorially*). Oh yes. We'll have the roolyeh-boolyeh, we will, in faith! And I never seen more stuff leave Bochtán for fair or market than I did this morning. Now, the brandy, and here's a drop to warm you up for now. Throw that back yeh. (*and she, too, has a secret drink for herself.*) An' twill be a blessin' after that bad harvest.

BINA (*drinks; then concerned*). But was I right do you think to give poor Tufty to Michael O'Donoghue to sell for me?

JOHN'S WIFE (*dandling the* INFANT). Deedydle-um deedydle
– And what else did you have to sell but the cow?!

BINA. But without himself knowing?

JOHN'S WIFE. Deedyle-um – And won't you have money in
your purse tonight like the others comin' home?

BINA. That's true. But he's lucid at times and then gets cross.

JOHN'S WIFE. Keep givin' him the laxatives. (*Writing.*)
Brandy. As much as he can eat of them.

*Outside, someone (COSTELLO) is arriving on a bicycle,
calling out a greeting.*

VOICE. There y'are, Josie!

JOHN'S WIFE. Whist! Is that . . .?

VOICE. Diabolically cold!

JOHN'S WIFE. Knuck-kaw och-khaw, Costello is back!

BINA. Costello, och-khaw!

JOHN'S WIFE. Now things'll start livenin' up in earnest –
knuch-kaw och-khaw!

BINA. Och khaw a-khaw!

JOSIE comes in.

BINA. Josie.

*He is the eccentric one; in middle thirties, skinny and severe-
looking. Unlike the others who are dressed against the
weather in layers of rough clothing, JOSIE's dress is sparse.
Shirt open at the neck, threadbare jacket and trousers, yet
showing no effects of the cold weather. He is carrying his
spade and a switch (or cane).*

JOHN'S WIFE. How yeh, Josie, is that Costello arriving?

JOSIE (*ignoring them, uttering his severe nasal sound*). Heh-hinnia!

BINA. Yeh didn't, Josie, think to bring my clock?

But JOSIE *has continued to the pub end of the shop to do his annual party piece.*

JOHN'S WIFE. Pleb! (*Calls.*) John!

BINA's eyes continuing after JOSIE, *then an imploring glance at* JOHN'S WIFE.

Oh he has it mended, he has it mended, all knows the amadán (*the fool*) has it mended these three days.

BINA (*has taken a few timid steps after* JOSIE). Because with the money I'll have from the sale of Tufty, you can charge me what you like, almost.

JOSIE (*warning her to keep away*). Heh-hinnia!

Because she is interfering with the business – his 'performance' – which he is now engaged in.

JOHN'S WIFE. Amadán! Look at him! Ride-the-Blind-Donkey, year after year. Leave him so (*for*) a while till he has a few pints and suitably placated, then I'll get John to speak to him. (*Calls.*) John! (*To* BINA.) Give me your pension book.

BINA. I think he has it (*the clock*) in his pocket.

JOHN'S WIFE. Lúdramán (*Josie is*)! Your pension money now is for last week's and I have them articles down with the others that are outstanding.

BINA. That will do, ma'am, I understand.

JOHN'S WIFE. Don't lose your book now.

And during this JOSIE *has commenced his party piece: he bridges the gap between two half-barrels with the spade, produces four flowers (or thistles) from his pocket and sets them erect, spaced apart, two on each barrel; then, standing astride the handle of the spade, he blindfolds himself; then, sitting on the spade handle, his two feet off the ground; then, maintaining this delicate balance, he urges on his 'donkey'; then, at some point, he makes four deft flicks of his switch taking the heads off the four flowers. His performance completed, he removes the blindfold, sets up four more flowers on the barrels and invites all present to have a go:*

JOSIE. Heh-hinnia?! . . . (*Quiet, sour satisfaction, to himself.*) Hin-ma-a-a-ay!

And he goes to the counter to rap severely on it. JOSIE's performance receives very little attention from the others present. The musicians conferring and playing trial snatches of music for themselves; a single philosophical groan from STEPHEN to the fire.

STEPHEN. Oh yis!

COSTELLO enters before JOSIE's performance is completed. He is a fine big man, a bit overweight, in his late thirties. The main feature of his character is his great laugh. (As is frequent in gatherings there is someone with an unusual sounding laugh, an infectious laugh.) COSTELLO's laugh explodes in the air – a great rumble – before going flying up into a cackling falsetto. Indeed, even at a distance, when people see or hear him approaching, an involuntary gurgle of laughter starts in their throats.

COSTELLO. Cold enough for ye, ladies!

BINA ⎱ Khaw och-khaw, Séamusheen a wockeen, God
⎰ bless, och-khaw!
JOHN'S WIFE ⎰ Knuck-uck-uck-khaw, hunucka huckina-
khaw, Costello!

COSTELLO. Rose, me flower! – An' fresh and well you're lookin', Bina!

BINA ⎱ Khaw-khaw-och-khaw!
JOHN'S WIFE ⎰ Knuck-uck-uck hunucka-khaw!

COSTELLO. Well, isn't it diabolically cold, ladies?

JOHN'S WIFE. How was the market, Jimmy?

COSTELLO (*evades the question*). How the man! (*To the infant.*) Isn't he gettin' awful big, God bless him? Jack Frost is comin' with a vengeance for you tonight – Or the Bogey Man maybe bejingoes! Well, someone is comin' anaways if you aren't good!

JOHN'S WIFE. Ye all sold well, Jimmy? –

COSTELLO (*leaving them*). Josie has the festivities started for us already. Good man, Josie! (*To BRIAN and STEPHEN.*) How the boys!

BRIAN (*a coughing/spitting gurgle*). A hacktha, Séamus, kuh-hucht!

STEPHEN. Oh yis. (*Philosophically to the fire – as throughout.*)

COSTELLO. Diabolically cold, boys!

JOHN'S WIFE (*calling again to kitchen*). John!

She is outside the counter now, the CHILD *following, and* BINA, *coming to the pub end.*

BRIAN. I seen yeh – A hacktha! – early enough on the road this mornin and I drawin' the bucket of water.

COSTELLO. Yeh did, Brian – wo-ho-ho! – an' you had the trouble crackin' the crust of ice in the barrel?

BRIAN. I had!

COSTELLO (*his falsetto giggle*). Hickle-ickle-ickle-ickle, you had.

BRIAN. Kuh-hucktha! – I had.

STEPHEN. Oh yis.

COSTELLO. Well you're still the sweetest flower, Rose!

JOHN'S WIFE (*harshly*). John, will yeh come out!

BRIAN. An' what's the news from the Big World!

COSTELLO. The Dutch has taken Holland!

Followed by a bellow of laughter that has the others – except
JOSIE *– laughing and chuckling.*

STEPHEN. Oh yis.

JOHN'S WIFE. But yeh sold well, Jimmy?

COSTELLO. No, but wait'll I tell ye. Coupla miles back the
road, comin' this ways to Bochtán, I seen the quarest couple.
A woman in black between the two hind shafts of a cart, bent
an' cráite as the Linaun Shee, an' she cryin' kinda strange-like
– Hah? – an' whingein' away to herself

BINA (*whispering*). Makin' this way?

COSTELLO. Makin' this way, Bina.

JOHN'S WIFE. Yes?

COSTELLO. An' her man, a class of a little gadhahaun – Jasus,
I nearly ran over him! The aul' bike (*outside*) – leadin' a
black horse by the winkers, an' – Hah? – 'Good evening' says
he up at me, smilin' in the corners of his mouth.

BINA (*whispering*). Good evening.

JOHN *is entering from the kitchen chewing the last of a meal
and licking his teeth. He is sixty, small, he is at least thirty
years his wife's senior, he has a stammer. If all were known
he is a very wealthy man. His moods can change rapidly. At
the moment he is very pleased with himself and, like the
others, he has great expectations of the evening and the party.*

COSTELLO. Now, Bina, 'Good evening', that's what he said –
Good man, John!

JOHN. You're here, K-Costello?

COSTELLO. I am, John –

JOHN'S WIFE. An' what was in the cart? –

COSTELLO. Throw us out an auld pint – I'm thinkin' something white.

JOHN (*in answer to* JOSIE's *rapping*). It's k-k-k-comin' Josie! Have you done your trick? (*Laughing to himself.*)

COSTELLO. Oh he has, he has.

JOHN. Ruh-ruh-ruh-Ride-the-Blind-Donkey. (*And laughs again.*)

COSTELLO. An' no bother to him, boy.

JOSIE (*inviting challengers*). Heh-hinnia?!

JOHN (*giving a pint to* JOSIE). No-no-no, there's no one to best yeh. And the first drink is on the house.

COSTELLO. Good man, John, yeh never failed us in anything.

JOHN (*filling* COSTELLO's *pint*). An' whuh-what're the musicians havin'?

FIDDLER. Whiskey.

JOHN. An'-an'-an' as m-much, nearly, as ye can drink of it, because that's the kind of man I am!

COSTELLO. Man, John! An' a drop of the hard tack too for me.

JOHN (*to* COSTELLO). Bring that (*whiskies*) over to them. (*To his wife.*) Stoke up the fire, bring in more turf. The night that's to be in it.

JOHN'S WIFE *stoking the fire.*

A drop of brandy, Bina?

BINA. Oh no-no-no, John, no.

JOHN. Oh n-no-no-no John no, but why a poor man like me, with a poor crayture of a wife like that has t-to be standin' ye drinks, I don't know.

*He winks at his wife's bottom – perhaps pats it – for the
amusement of the others. Curiously, in this case, COSTELLO
is not amused and his action is protective of the young
woman.*

COSTELLO. Here, Rose, let me do that: you don't know how
to build a decent fire.

JOHN'S WIFE *now understands what the chuckling is about.*

JOHN'S WIFE. Thanks, Jimmy. (*then she glares at* JOHN *and
imitates his stammer.*) Duh-duh-duh-duh-duh! (*Defiantly gets
a drink for herself; to the musicians.*) F-f-fire away! Let the p-
p-party buh-buh-buh-begin!

JOHN (*flustered for a moment*). But-but-but, see what good the
p-pensions will do ye, stuck in the mattresses when ye're all
d-dead. Whuh-when ye're dead.

COSTELLO (*when he gets his pint*). A toast! To honest John
Mahony. Drink to his health or else, says he, on the crown of
yere heads, arses up in the air, as sure as be damned, it's in
hell ye shall be!

A rumble of laughter from COSTELLO, *the others chuckling,
as they raise their glasses.*

JOHN. N-not at-at-at (*all*) – But thanks, thanks, thank ye all
now.

Music continues.

You wor (*were*) in ch-Tuam, K-Costello?

COSTELLO. I was in Tuam, John.

JOHN'S WIFE. You wor, Jimmy.

COSTELLO. I was, Rose.

BINA (*smiling her expectation*). An' how was it?

COSTELLO. Well, not tellin' ye a word of a lie now, but 'twas deadly.

Silence.

JOHN'S WIFE. Ara stop. (*Meaning that he is joking.*)

But there is no smile from COSTELLO.

BINA (*an awed whisper*). Ory!

JOHN'S WIFE. Did yeh hear?

JOHN *now tight-lipped, a frown deepening on his brow.*

STEPHEN. Oh yis.

JOHN'S WIFE (*whispering*). Well, d'yeh tell me so?

COSTELLO. I do tell yeh so.

JOHN'S WIFE. No.

COSTELLO. Talkin' about a Maragadh Mór?! – I never in all me born days seen likes or light of it.

JOHN. J-Jasus Christ!

COSTELLO *nods solemnly.*

BRIAN. Hah?

JOHN. An'-an'-an' look at all the stock I bought in for the Christmas!

JOHN'S WIFE (*whispering*). Yis?

COSTELLO. Firkins of butter an' cheese be the hundredweight, says he! Ducks, geese, chickens, bonhams and! (*He claps his mouth shut.*) Geese?! Geese says he!? There was hundreds of them! There was hundreds upon hundreds of thousands of them! The ground I tell ye was white with them!

BINA. White with them

JOHN. They went ch-cheap then?

COSTELLO. Cheap then?! –

JOHN. Sis-sis-stop your rappin' there now, Josie, or you won't get as much as a p-p-pint of water here tonight! –

COSTELLO. Cheap then?! –

JOSIE (*he has the money*). Heh-hinnia-money! –

JOHN (*filling another pint for* JOSIE). Ch-ch-ch-ch-cheap then – (*To* JOSIE.) Stop! – ch-cheap then, isn't that what I said? ch-cheap then!

COSTELLO. Sure you couldn't give them away sure!

JOHN (*planking a pint in front of* JOSIE). Now am I f-f-f-friggin f-fillin' it f-fast enough for yeh?

JOSIE. Heh-hinnia! (*Planking down his coin.*)

COSTELLO. Sure the sight of so many ducks an' geese an' chickens an' what-nots, sure all the people could do was stand an' stare!

BINA. They were puzzled.

JOHN *is sighing heavily through his nose, trying to think how to turn misfortune into fortune.*

JOHN (*to musicians*). Stop, will ye!

COSTELLO. Can't ye play something nice an' – delicate – for the decent man (*that*) hired ye. An' the small one yeh promised me, John.

JOHN. F-f-frig the small one! Now d'yeh know?

The musicians have been conferring and now start to play 'Hard Times' ('*tis the sad sigh of the weary*').

(*To himself.*) So no one sis-sold nothin'.

BINA (*to herself*). Aw Lord no!

COSTELLO (*rooting in his pockets for coins*). Oh well, if you're (JOHN *is.*) goin' back on your word. But I'm telling yeh, Napoleon Bonaparte wouldn't have said no to all the provisions goin a-begging in that town of Tuam today.

JOHN (*irritably, his attempt to think matters out being interrupted*). Hah?

COSTELLO. On his retreat from Moscow sure.

JOHN. J-J-Jesus, I'm mythered! (*His head is confused.*)

COSTELLO. Or Josephine – Wuw! – neither. (*And another rumble of laughter.*)

JOHN (*angrily*). But you sis-sold all the r-rabbits, did yeh, K-Costello?

COSTELLO (*slight hesitation*). Aw –

JOHN. Aw! – Aw!

COSTELLO. Oh, I sold, oh I did, did! – Oh, on me solemn-'n-dyin' oath, every man-jack-rabbit of them! Luck again, men!

BINA. An Tufty?

JOHN. Yeh-yeh-yeh codjer yeh! (*Walking away to his office, followed by his WIFE.*) An' to be swearin' oaths like that!

COSTELLO. Ary what harm.

BRIAN. An' who else was in it from Bochtán, Séamus?

COSTELLO. Sure everyone, sure! The Kemples, Martin John and Anthony.

BRIAN. Pigs they had?

COSTELLO. Pigs, yes, bonavs. (*Bonhams.*)

BRIAN. An' Tomás Rua.

COSTELLO. An' Tomás.

STEPHEN (*groans to fire, funereally*). Cabbage plants.

COSTELLO. Cabbage plants, to be sure, yes, what else.

STEPHEN. An' scollops.

COSTELLO. An' the Sheridans, the Garas, Sheehans, Mick Shlevin, Pat Shaughnessy, the O'Connors.

BINA. Michael O'Donoghue? I gave him the cow to sell for me.

COSTELLO. Hah? Oh, well, yes. I passed the two of them on the road, Michael an' Tufty. Ara what, Bina, wasn't she only a pet to yeh? Sorrier ye'd be if yeh sold her.

BRIAN. They'll all be here soon.

COSTELLO. No. But home, and with heads bent, they'll be goin'.

During the above, JOHN'S WIFE *has been whispering to* JOHN *in his office at the other end of the shop;* JOHN *wincing and sighing and gesturing his frustration.*

JOHN. J-J-Jasus! . . . Look it, woman! . . . Pestered! . . . F-f-f-frig the friggin' clock! (*But he is returning to the pub end to engage with* COSTELLO *and* JOSIE. *To his* WIFE.) An look at the way you have the ch-child scattered under my feet! (*To* COSTELLO.) K-k-k-codjer – you're-you're-you're only a fool – P-p-p-people laughin' at the sight of yeh! –

COSTELLO. What did I – ? (*do*)

JOHN (*to* JOSIE). An'-an' you, yeh-yeh-yeh dunce, yeh-yeh thick pleb, yeh-yeh-yeh jolter-headed gob-shite! – Give that woman back her K-clock!

JOSIE. Heh-hinnia!

JOHN. K-cobblin, at it these three months –

JOSIE (*whose business is that?*). Hinnia-whose-business? –

JOHN. The whole country knowin' you have it m-mended.

COSTELLO. Good man, Josie, you have it well-tested now.

JOHN'S WIFE. He has it in his pocket.

JOSIE (*clasping/protecting his pocket*). Heh-hinnia!

JOHN. J-J-Jasus! – (*Catches* JOSIE.)

BRIAN ⎫ Do, Josie, a mac, give it back —
JOHN ⎬ He-he-he has — in his pocket! —
JOHN'S WIFE ⎭ She's lost without it —

JOHN. Jasus, I can hear the tick! —

BINA. I miss the tick —

JOHN. Walkin' round like a t-time-bomb! —

JOSIE. Heh-hinnia! — (*He has broken free.*) Hin-money!

BINA. I've no money to pay him now —

JOHN'S WIFE. John'll pay him for yeh.

JOHN. J-Jasus, John'll pay! Sh-Stephen! —

JOHN'S WIFE. What'll it cost but the bob or two?

JOHN (*to* WIFE). Will you get the child in! Will you speak to him, Stephen? You're his f-f-father, aren't yeh? — if y'are!

Old STEPHEN *looks up from the fire — possibly for the first time — alarmed at the suggestion of speaking to his son,* JOSIE.

JOSIE (*at* STEPHEN). Heh-hinnia!

JOHN (*en-route to his office*). Sis-sis-sort it out for yereselves then, but th-the roof is gone from over my head! An lookit — (*Returning with his big ledger.*) Lookit! Not a one of ye hasn't his or her name down here in red writin'. J-Jasus every time I look at it I see the Poor House waiting for me!

JOHN'S WIFE (*taking the* INFANT *into the kitchen*). You're gettin' too old-fashioned entirely — Stop your whingein' now or you'll know what you'll get from me — in there with yeh!

JOHN (*returning*). An'-an'-an' some of ye goin' round like buh-big ranchers — (*To musicians.*) Frig 'Moonlight in Mayo'!

The musicians stop playing 'Hard Times'.

(*To* COSTELLO.) With fields to burn — Ye don't know what to do with them, overrun with weeds. The g-grandest humour till yeh came in that door, Costello, now I'd f-f-fight with St. Peter!

COSTELLO. But what did I —

JOHN. Oh but-but-but, K-Costello yourself! Will you sell me that field I was askin' about?

COSTELLO. I won't.

JOHN. Yeh-yeh won't, an'-an' I'm expected to keep fillin' you up with porter. The village fool, you're only a rake, an' a scavenger. But J-J-John'll do this, J-John'll do that, John'll keep ye all g-g-g-goin!

BRIAN. Whist!

And they are all now listening to a cart stopping on the road outside.

BINA. Is it the strange creatures you met on the road, Séamus?

STEPHEN (*groans to the fire*). 'Tis the wheels of Kemples' ass an' cart.

COSTELLO. 'Tis.

VOICE (MARTIN JOHN's). I'll see yeh in a minute then!

The cart moving off.

MARTIN JOHN *comes in. He is in his early twenties.* (ANTHONY *who comes in later is a couple of years younger.*) *The day's disaster on* MARTIN JOHN's *face.*

JOHN. You 'rived in time for the party, Martin John. Ye have yere party there now with what's in front of ye. (*He is moving off; he turns back.*) Well, I'm tellin' ye all now, a thief of a Christmas we're all goin' t'have!

He goes to his office, and stands there, his hand resting on his holy book, the ledger.

MARTIN JOHN (*a muted greeting*). Men!

Muted replies.

COSTELLO. Well, I don't know . . . One yeh sold?

MARTIN JOHN. Two. (*He is counting his pittance of money.*)

JOSIE (*challenging* MARTIN JOHN *to Ride-the-Blind-Donkey*). Heh-hinnia?

COSTELLO. Stop, Josie! Give us a song, Bina. (*He winks at* JOSIE's *back suggesting to her a song might soften* JOSIE.) Girl on yeh!

BINA *starts to sing* 'The Swanee River'. *The musicians to accompany her.*

BINA. 'Way down upon the Swanee River, far, far, away . . . (*Etc.*)

COSTELLO (*as she sings; to* MARTIN JOHN). Try a deal with himself (JOHN) for the bonavs, tell him you'll over-winter them for him. An' what else can we do?! Christmas next Tuesday, bejingoes! An' we'll have the game of cards.

JOSIE (*to* MARTIN JOHN). Hinnia?

COSTELLO (*to* MARTIN JOHN). Go on. (*To* JOSIE.) Maybe Anthony'd challenge yeh when he comes in.

MARTIN JOHN *has gone to* JOHN *and we see him whispering like a penitent and demonstrating on his fingers his assets and prospects. And, meanwhile,* COSTELLO *is searching the mantelpiece and looking over the counter for the pack of cards.*

Good girl, Bina! 'When I was playing with my brother.' Right, men, Spoil Five, First Fifteen or A Hundred and Ten? – Did anyone see the – Where's the pack of cards, John?

JOHN (*calls back*). The-the child et (*ate*) them! Now d'yeh know!

BRIAN (*whispering*). He's not givin' them out.

COSTELLO. But sure he didn't ate (*eat*) them all?!

JOHN. N-near choked himself! (*and continues sighing and shaking his head to* MARTIN JOHN.)

BINA *finishes her song. They forget to applaud her.*

COSTELLO (*sighs*). Well, indeed. I do not know.

STEPHEN. And a long winter ahead.

BRIAN. Cuh-huchta-hachtha!

JOSIE (*quietly*). Heh-hinnia!

STEPHEN. Oh yis.

COSTELLO. 'The bright day is done,' he says, 'and we are for the dark.' Oh, but something'll turn up yet.

TOMÁS RUA, *a one-armed man, about fifty has entered accompanied by his daughter* PEGGY, *a large-eyed, comsumptive-looking girl.*

TOMÁS. Could I see yeh for a minute, John, when you're ready?

He continues to the pub end where he is greeted. He merely nods in reply to the greetings; it is obvious that he is in poor straits.

COSTELLO. Tomás.

BRIAN. Tomás, a mac.

COSTELLO. A bad market. And pretty Peggy! Ye'll give us a song, Peggy! In a while then maybe.

STEPHEN (*unaware of* TOMÁS's – *or anyone's presence*) An' wasn't Tomás Rua the foolish man thinkin' cabbage plants an' scallops suitable cargo for the Christmas market.

JOHN's *eyes have shown an interest in* TOMÁS RUA; *he is eager to get away from* MARTIN JOHN *and, simultaneous with the above he has begun making his way to pub end.*

MARTIN JOHN. Aw but not for that price – !

JOHN. L-l-look, give me t-time to think now, Martin John –

MARTIN JOHN	An' weren't yeh thinkin' of buildin' an extension –
JOHN	An' maybe with the help of God –

MARTIN JOHN	Anthony no more than myself is handy an' could –
JOHN	I'll – lookit – highest regard for the Kemples always but excuse me now, Martin John, but-but-but! (*He leaves* MARTIN JOHN; *he gives a sweet to* PEGGY.) Now, Peggy, that's for you. (*He gives the pack of cards to* COSTELLO.) Ye'd think 'twas a k-k-k-casino. Yeh wanted a word, Tomás? (*Leading* TOMÁS RUA *to the office.*) D-did ye sis-see a doctor for her like I advised?

And they commence whispering and dealing at JOHN's *little office.*

COSTELLO (*counting the cards*). How'd yeh get on?

MARTIN JOHN *sighs in frustration.*

He'll see? He will. Jasus, they're well chewed alright. And if he had my bottom field that butts his, an' the other half of Tomás Rua's little place on the other side of him . . . (*To the cards.*) Hah? Thirty-nine cards out of a pack of fifty-two! An' the best eatin' was in the hearts. (*He throws the cards away.*) We're not goin' to prosper in this diversion this night. Oh, but the night will send us something yet, won't it, Peggy?

ANTHONY *is coming in backwards: he remains with his head poking out the door for a moment. The rattling and creaking of a horse and cart approaching.*

BRIAN. Whist!

BINA. Michael O'Donoghue, is it, that's in it an' –

COSTELLO. Shh!

JOHN'S WIFE enters with an armful of turf and is stopped by the silence.

STEPHEN (*to the fire*). 'Tis strangers.

MARTIN JOHN. Did yeh pass them, Séamus? – The strangers.

COSTELLO. The Linaun Shee? – I told them all about it – an' the little gadhahaun of a man with her. (*He winks at the* KEMPLES.)

ANTHONY (*peeping out the window*). They're stoppin'. They're lookin' up at Loughran's hill.

COSTELLO. They won't get up it.

Others peeping out the window.

ANTHONY. They're lookin' back the road they came.

COSTELLO. They won't get back it. (*Winks at* MARTIN JOHN *again.*)

MARTIN JOHN. Lord Christ tonight an' Jasus, but we didn't know in the distance what at all on earth was in it, was dazzlin in the dip ablow longside Patch Curran's place!

COSTELLO. Even th'aul ass himself was frikened, Martin John?

MARTIN JOHN. An' startin' for to balk!

ANTHONY. An' me thinkin' 'twas the Divil ablow, his forges started eruptin'!

COSTELLO (*mock urgency*). With the help of God they'll not come in here, Josie! – An' the chains, Martin John?

MARTIN JOHN. An the chains – Oh Jasus! – rattlin', Josie!

JOSIE. Heh-hinnia! –

JOHN'S WIFE. An' what was it it was in it?

MARTIN JOHN. An' was judgement come to our souls? – Jasus!

COSTELLO (*at the window*). Jasus, he's smilin' again on the corners of his mouth – he's lookin' this way!

COSTELLO *and* MARTIN JOHN *have turned away to hide their laughter. They are blackguarding/frightening the others, but they are also frightening themselves.*

JOHN'S WIFE. But what at all in heaven or earth was dazzlin' ye?

BRIAN. Kuh-hucktha!

STEPHEN. 'Twas the showers of sparks risin' from the horse's hooves slippin'.

JOHN'S WIFE (*dismissing it all*). Ara stop! (*And stacking turf by the fire.*)

BINA (*whispering*). Maybe it was more?

MARTIN JOHN. Well, I don't know – And they wor quiet, Anthony? – but the bonavs that were sleepin' of a sudden started screechin'.

BINA. Now.

COSTELLO. Now, Bina. A quare, strange year we had of it, and could this be the explanation?

STEPHEN. A heavy horse.

ANTHONY. They're roundin' the gable, man, goin' into the yard!

BRIAN. A-hacktha! – Aw but ye stopped?

COSTELLO. They were afeared not to.

MARTIN JOHN. An' near destroyed pull an' pushin' horse an' cart up the hill.

JOHN'S WIFE. An' who are they?

MARTIN JOHN. Sure we didn't have wind to ask them.

COSTELLO. Nor heart after the encounter? Well, I don't like it, Josie. (*Back to* MARTIN JOHN.) Here, give me your money, I'll pool it with mine.

MARTIN JOHN *is reluctant, wondering is he being conned, but he gives his money to* COSTELLO.

JOSIE. Heh-hinnia!

COSTELLO. We need fortifications. (*Calls.*) John!

JOHN *is concluding his business with the downcast* TOMÁS RUA: *a deal has not been struck, but* JOHN's *return to good form suggests that he is optimistic. They are returning to the pub end,* TOMÁS RUA *to sit beside his daughter and, unconsciously, commence thumping his knee at his plight,* JOHN *to serve drinks.*

JOHN. Th-think it over now, Tomás. No one is r-rushin' yeh. An' I always had the highest regard for your in-in-in-intelligence. (*To* COSTELLO.) An' if you, yeh-yeh playboy, had the sense you'd be considerin' too what thum-thum-Tomás Rua is goin' to do.

COSTELLO. A pint an' a small one, John, for me – The money is there! – and a pint for Martin John and Anthony.

JOHN'S WIFE. There's two strangers in the yard –

JOHN. Take that (*a whisky*) over to Tomás — An'-an'-an' l-leave your knee along now Tomás! You're goin' to do the right an' p-p-proper thing. On the house (*the whisky is*) an'-an'-an' the bottle of minerals for that grand little daughter of his, the creature.

JOHNS WIFE. Two quare strangers —

JOHN. I heard. An' hoo-hoo-hoo whoever they are, an' whuh-whuh-whuh whatever they are, an' wheh-wheh-wheh —

COSTELLO. Wherever they're goin', they'll not get there, John, the night that's in it — throw me out the small one — nor to the top of the Himalayas of India neither — thank you — not even if they had a motor car!

STEPHEN. Oh yis: you can't bate (*beat*) the aul' ass all the same.

COSTELLO. Well, here's health and bright glory to us all, and a happy and holy . . .

The strangers enter.

Well, here's to the hand that made the ball that shot Lord Leitrim of Donegal!

The strangers stand in the doorway (the back door from the yard). The woman, head bowed, behind her husband, to conceal the fact that she has been crying. The STRANGER is a small man, in his sixties. He is wearing a cap and the usual peasant dress; a black diamond stitched on his sleeve: a symbol that he is in mourning. There is a quiet dignity and politeness about him; and the 'smiles' on the corners of his mouth suggest a quiet defiance of adversity as well as a fatalistic streak. He has been dogged by misfortune but he has always tried to contain himself. His WIFE is fiftyish (or in her forties, but she looks older). A black shawl over her head, falling on to and around the shoulders of a black overcoat. At times when she draws the shawl about her we see that she has three sticks of rock (sweets) in her hand.

STRANGER (*quietly*). God bless all here. (*Not quite distinguishable.*)

BINA (*whispering*). What did the gadahaun say?

BRIAN. Kuh-hacktha! (*Coughs a reply to the strangers.*)

JOSIE (*quietly, to himself*). Heh-hinnia!

The STRANGER *indicates a seat to his* WIFE *in a corner. An involuntary sob from* WIFE. *The* STRANGER *smiles at the locals again and nods at them.*

COSTELLO *and* MARTIN JOHN *nod back.*

JOHN'S WIFE. What has she in her hand?

JOHN (*coming out of his frowning reverie*). Oh k-k-come on, let ye – (*To strangers.*) God bless ye, ye're welcome! – (*To his wife.*) Sis-sweets, now d'yeh know?! (*To the others who are still gawking at the strangers.*) Have ye no m-manners? Yid (*you would*) think 'twas Ros-Roscommon people ye were!

COSTELLO (*slagging*). D'ye know no better?! (*Quietly to* JOSIE.) Though I don't like it. Still, your turn, give us that song of yours, 'The Boston Burglar', Josie!

JOHN'S WIFE. Sweets?

JOSIE (*to himself*). Heh-hinnia!

JOHN. Sis-sis-sweets, sweets, is your curiosity satisfied now? (*At the same time telling her where her place is: the kitchen.*)

COSTELLO (*raising his fresh pint*). Luck, men!

MARTIN JOHN. Good luck! –

ANTHONY. Good luck! –

COSTELLO. Luck! (*And he rumbles a laugh to himself.*)

The STRANGER *registers a mild interest in* COSTELLO, *as if trying to remember something. Now he is inclining his head towards his* WIFE *to hear the better what she is whispering.*

STRANGER'S WIFE. Misfortunes.

STRANGER *takes a deep breath but contains it.*

And I caught Tom the other evening playing with the mangler, his feet dancin' in the cup.

STRANGER. Not at all, not at all.

STRANGER'S WIFE. And won't they have to light the lamp? The paraffin.

STRANGER. Not at all, not at all.

STRANGER'S WIFE. And the fox on the prowl, sure they'll not think to secure the hens.

STRANGER. Isn't Mary a big girl now and well able to look after the other two.

STRANGER'S WIFE. An won't they –

STRANGER. Stop, woman! . . . Or May Glynn'll be lookin' in on them.

STRANGER'S WIFE. Three miles across fields.

STRANGER. Or someone else then. (*He contains another sigh.*)

STRANGER'S WIFE. And sure we told them for sure we'd be home before dark.

STRANGER (*unconsciously*). Misfortunes. (STRANGER *stands abruptly, betraying an inner concern and a turbulence, but he controls himself again and sits.*) Not at all, not at all. (*But he is up again and he goes to the counter.*)

Overlapping the above, the locals have been continuing.

ANTHONY. But did yeh see all the fowl?

COSTELLO. The cluckin' an' the quackin' an' the cacklin' of them –

MARTIN JOHN. An the screechin' an' the squealin' of all the pigs in the bonav-market!

COSTELLO. Oh, a lota noise an' little wool as Peadar Dall McKenny said shearin' the pig!

Another rumble of laughter. JOHN *has come to serve the*
STRANGER.

JOHN. That's a bad night outside, Mister.

STRANGER. It is. (*But he is listening to* COSTELLO *again.*) It
is, a bad night.

JOHN. Whuh-what'll you be havin'?

STRANGER. We can't get up the hill.

JOHN. I understand.

STRANGER. I put my horse and cart into one of your stables.

JOHN. An' you're welcome.

STRANGER. Thank you. Till I see what to do.

JOHN. You'll be h-havin' something?

STRANGER. A small whiskey, if you please, and a drop of port
wine.

JOHN (*getting drinks*). The frost is determined to make a night
of it?!

BRIAN. Behell I don't know: comin' on duskess there was a
fine roll of cloud over in the west and if you got the bit of a
breeze at all I'm thinkin' you'd soon see a thaw.

COSTELLO. 'Deed yeh won't see any thaw – nor before
Christmas, or the new Year. What harm! 'Oh I am a bold
bachelor aisy an' free, both city an' country is aiqual (*equal*)
to me!'

Another rumble of laughter from COSTELLO *and he has the
others laughing.*

The STRANGER *is listening quietly to them.*

BRIAN. Come on, Anthony, aren't yeh goin' to challenge Josie
to ride that donkey there?

ANTHONY *has a go at Ride-the-Blind-Donkey. Ad-libs, etc. During this* JOHN *brings drinks to the* STRANGER.

JOHN. Now, Mister.

STRANGER. Thank you.

The STRANGER *takes the drinks to his* WIFE. WIFE *now starts to cry, her head turned in and out of the corner.*

JOHN. Not at all, not at all –

STRANGER'S WIFE. An' won't they have to feed themselves? –

STRANGER (*about to sit*). Stop will ye! –

STRANGER'S WIFE. Put themselves to bed –

STRANGER. What can I do? –

STRANGER'S WIFE. Tom's bad chest.

STRANGER. At the end of my tether.

There is nothing he can do for her so he goes to a quiet spot at the counter. COSTELLO'*s laughter dominating at* ANTHONY'*s efforts to Ride-the-Blind-Donkey.*

JOHN (*joins* STRANGER). Yeh have a distance to go, Mister.

STRANGER. I have.

JOHN. You have. Hah?

STRANGER (*puzzling to himself*). Would that big man down there be a man be the name of Costello?

JOHN. Th-th-that's who he is. Hah?

STRANGER, *frowning, nods solemnly.*

Hah? D'yeh know him?

STRANGER. No.

JOHN. Hah?

STRANGER. No. But that's a fine laugh?

JOHN. Oh, 'tis a fine laugh right enough.

STRANGER. 'Tis.

JOHN. Hah?

STRANGER. I heard that laugh a wintry day the likes of this, a few years back, across the market square in Ballindine.

JOHN. You did.

STRANGER. I did. And I had to ask a man who he was.

JOHN. Yeh had.

STRANGER *nods but he is still puzzled by a thought which hasn't yet reached the senses.*

Yis?

Then the STRANGER's *frown disappears, he chuckles to himself, then he looks up at* JOHN, *sadly, the two little smiles on the corners of his mouth.*

STRANGER. Well, I'm a better laugher than your Costello.

JOHN's *surprise for a moment, then he nods, once, solemnly. Then he calls:*

JOHN. K-K-K-Costello! . . . Sh-Séamus! Will yeh come down a minute.

COSTELLO (*joining them*). Hah? (JOHN *directs his attention to the* STRANGER.) Hah? (*but the* STRANGER's *eyes are still fixed on* JOHN; *to* JOHN.) Hah?

But JOHN *refers* COSTELLO *back to the* STRANGER *again as he takes a step backwards to get out of the* STRANGER's *line of vision and to declare his neutrality in the matter.* COSTELLO's *head now turning from* JOHN *to* STRANGER *and growing bewildered.*

Hah? Hah? Hah? Hah?

STRANGER (*eyes straight ahead*). How d'yeh do, Mr Costello?

COSTELLO (*to* STRANGER). Hah?! (*He looks at* JOHN.)

JOHN (*puffing a tuneless whistle at the ceiling*). Phuh-phuh phuh-phuh . . .

COSTELLO. I'm very well, thanking you!

STRANGER. I'm Séamus O'Toole.

COSTELLO's *head from* STRANGER *to* JOHN *again.*

JOHN. Oh – Phuh phuh phuh – M-m-m-mister K-Costello's a Séamus too – phuh-phuh-phuh.

STRANGER. I know that. But I'm a better laugher than 'm.

COSTELLO *gurgles an incredulous laugh in his throat.*

STRANGER (*chuckles in reply*). Heh-heh-heh-heh, heh-heh-heh-heh!

COSTELLO (*laughing in his throat again, then breaking off to declare*). He says, he says, he says to me, he's a better! (*He claps his mouth shut, discovering suddenly that he is angry.*) Ara phat?! ('What.' *And skipping backwards and forwards like a man preparing to fight.*)

The STRANGER *chuckles.*

He says, he says, he says to me (*that*) he's a better laugher than me!

The locals have never heard the likes, nor do they know how to deal with it, so things are looking dangerous. They start to make small angry sounds in their throats, not knowing quite why.

Ara, give me a pint outa that! (*As he starts back to his place, sweeping people out of his way, then changes his mind suddenly and swivels about. He sets himself squarely on his feet, head swung upwards, mouth open and utters a strange-sounding bellow. But it is forced, it has no mirth, and he claps his mouth shut, snorts in frustration and goes back to the counter, his back to the others.*)

The STRANGER *chuckles again, this time at himself, at the outrageous idea that came into his head and he returns to his* WIFE.

The others, glancing from one to the other, from the STRANGER *to* COSTELLO - *and seeing* COSTELLO's *upset – are making further angry noises. And even* JOSIE, *who usually remains aloof, does a circle of the floor, calling nasally at the* STRANGER –

JOSIE. Heh-hinnia!

COSTELLO (*holding up his empty glass*). John! – (It's) S'alright, lads. Pint for myself, Martin John and Anthony! (*To* JOHN.) S'alright, isn't it? I'll find the money for the drink – somewhere. Maybe – you'd never know – we might do a deal about that bottom field of mine yet. And one for Josie! S'alright, s'alright, I'm not a bit upset. (*Starts singing.*) 'I was born an' reared in Boston, a place you all –' And one for Bina! – 'know well'. But isn't it diabolically cold, men? 'Brought up by honest parents, the truth to ye I'll tell; brought up by – 'Come on, Bina! – 'honest parents and reared most tenderly, till I became –' Come on Bina! –

JOSIE (*singing tremulously, off key, nasally*). 'Till I became a sporting lad –'

COSTELLO } Good girl, Bina! 'At the age of twenty-three' –
JOSIE   } 'At the age of twenty-three' –

BINA (*starts singing*). 'Way down upon the Swanee River –'

JOSIE   } 'My character was broken – '
BINA   } 'Far, far away –'
COSTELLO } Oh sorry, Josie, that's your song. 'Let us pause in life's pleasures –' ('*Hard Times*'.)

JOSIE   } 'And I was sent to jail – '
BINA   } 'That's where my heart is longing ever – '
COSTELLO } Good on ye, cas amach é! – 'And count its many tears – '

The musicians are trying to complement. JOSIE, BINA *and* COSTELLO *are now singing three different songs simultaneously.*

JOSIE	'My friends and parents did their best – '
BINA	'That's where I long to stay – '
COSTELLO	'Hard times, hard times come again no more – '

JOSIE	'For to get me out on bail –'
BINA	'All the world is sad and weary –'
COSTELLO	'Many days you have lingered –'

JOSIE	'But the jury found me guilty –'
BINA	'Everywhere I roam –'
COSTELLO	'Oh hard times come again no more –' Thanks, John. (*for a fresh pint.*)

JOSIE	'And the clerk he wrote it down –'
BINA	'Oh, darkie, how my heart grows weary –'
COSTELLO	''Tis the sad cry of the weary – ' Style! –

JOSIE	'For the breaking of the Union Bank –'
BINA	'Far from the old folks at home –'
COSTELLO	'Hard times, hard times, come again no more –'

JOSIE	'I can see my dear old father standing at the door–'
BINA	'When I was playing with my brother –'
COSTELLO	'Many days you have lingered – ' Luck, men!

JOSIE	'Likewise my dear old mother, she was tearing out her hair –'
BINA	'Happy was I, still longing for the old plantation–'
COSTELLO	(*talking to himself*). Hah?. . .Hah?. . .Hah?

JOSIE	'She was tearing out her old grey locks –'
BINA	'Still longing for the old plantation –'
COSTELLO	'Oh hard times come again no more –'

JOSIE	'Crying John, my son, what have you done –'
BINA	'There let me live or die.'
COSTELLO	'Hat?! (*'what,' angrily to himself*)

BINA *stops.* COSTELLO *is striding to the strangers.* JOSIE *continues singing for a few more seconds.*

JOSIE. 'To be sent to Charles Town. I was born and reared in Boston . . . '

The strangers have been conferring and the STRANGER *has risen to go out and check the weather.*

COSTELLO. Excuse me a minute, Mister – Excuse me there a minute now, but what did you say to me there a minute ago? That you're a better laugher than me, is it?

STRANGER (*a silent*). No. (*And is making for the door again.*)

COSTELLO. No! No! – Excuse me! That you're the better laugher is it?

STRANGER. No.

COSTELLO. Well, would you care to put a small bet on it?

STRANGER. No.

COSTELLO. But you're challe'gin' me, challe'gin' me, challe'gin' me, y'are!

STRANGER. No.

MARTIN JOHN	He is, he is, he is, he is, he is!
ANTHONY	An' look at him smilin'! –
JOSIE	Heh-hinnia?! –
STRANGER	No! No! . .
COSTELLO	Hah?

JOHN. Ary sh-sh-sh-sure you're not, Mister? –

COSTELLO. 'Hat?! (*what?!*) –

MARTIN JOHN. He is, to be sure – Jasus! –

STRANGER. No. –

JOSIE. Challe'gin, – heh-hinn – yeh! –

COSTELLO. Is it me to be afraid of yeh – or the likes of yeh – or either of ye – yeh gadahaun yeh?! –

OTHERS (*shouting*). He is, he is, Séamus, challe'gin' yeh –

JOHN. A-a-aisy! –

COSTELLO. Hah?! –

STRANGER (*quietly*). No. 'Twas only a notion. (*And he winks up at* COSTELLO *so that* COSTELLO *will understand the better and he adds his chuckle.*) Heh-heh-heh, heh-heh-heh.

COSTELLO *half-understanding.*

Just goin' out to check the weather.

But a melée has started. They are milling round the strangers. JOHN'S WIFE *and* CHILD *are out from the kitchen again.*

OTHERS	He is, he is, Costello! –
JOSIE	Heh-hinnia! (*Etc.*) –
ANTHONY	Can't yeh hear him – 'Heh-heh-heh, heh-heh-heh'! –
JOHN	D-Didn't the man say he's not?! –
MARTIN JOHN	Stand where y'are, mister! – Jasus! –
BINA	An' bad cess to ye – an' to the two of ye! –
MARTIN JOHN	Bochtán, up Bochtán, Bochtán forever! –
JOHN	A-aisy, a-aisy! – (*to his wife.*) Will yeh-yeh-yeh look to the child – (*to the others.*) Will ye-ye stop will ye!

COSTELLO (*roars*). Silence!

He throws JOSIE *back.*

BINA. The clock! (*Concerned for her clock in* JOSIE's *pocket.*)

COSTELLO. Till I think . . . You're not? (STRANGER *shakes his head.*) That's alright then. My decree: it's all over.

JOHN. An'-an' that's my decree too. 'Tis all over! N-now d'ye know?

COSTELLO (*drinking*). Luck men!

STEPHEN (*to the fire*). Oh yis: 'tis not all over.

Now that they have returned to their places, we see the STRANGER'S WIFE, face aghast, on her knees, looking at the floor. In the jostling and pushing the three sticks of rock (the sweets) were knocked out of her hand and trampled underfoot. She picks up crumbs of the sweets and looks at them – dust.

STRANGER'S WIFE. The sweets! (*A whisper.*)

Silence.

JOHN. Whuh-whuh-what's up with yeh, m-ma'am?

STRANGER'S WIFE (*whispers*). The children! My grandchildren! The children that death left in my care!

JOHN. . . . Hah?

STRANGER *who has been making for the door is coming back to her.*

STRANGER'S WIFE (*to herself*). I'll renege matters no longer.

STRANGER (*helping her to her feet*). Shhhh!

STRANGER'S WIFE (*shakes off his hands; shouts*). Och hona-ho 'gus hah-haa!

STRANGER. Shh, woman!

STRANGER'S WIFE (*to* JOHN.) You can decree! – (*To* COSTELLO.) You can decree! – (*To her husband.*) All others can decree! but I'll-bear-matters-no-longer! (*To* COSTELLO.) Och hona-ho 'gus hah-haa! He's challe'gin' yeh.

Some of them are frightened of her, including COSTELLO.

(*To her husband, quietly.*) Well then? (*And she sits.*)

COSTELLO (*to* STRANGER, *who is already standing*). Stand up then. (*To the others.*) Scaith siar uaim! – We'll see then – clear back off the floor! 'Scuse me a minute. (*He coughs in preparation.*) A-wuffa-hachkht! (*Puts a spit in one hand, then one in the other and ponders a third that he sends to the floor; opens his mouth: a sudden thought and he claps his mouth shut.*) What's the topic?

JOHN (*to himself*). J-Jasus Christ!

COSTELLO. The topic, the topic to launch us . . . Then we'll have to do without one. (*He goes through the motions of preparation but claps his mouth shut again.*) Wait a minute. Who's to go first?

MARTIN JOHN *tosses a coin in the air.*

MARTIN JOHN. Cry. (*To the contestants.*)

COSTELLO. Harps, sure, harps.

MARTIN JOHN. Harps. (*To* STRANGER.) Heads to go first.

STRANGER *looks at his* WIFE. *She refuses to look at him.*

STRANGER. 'Scuse me too. (*He looks at the floor, the two fatalistic smiles appearing on the corners of his mouth. He coughs – making COSTELLO stiffen – and looks up. Then, easy and gentle, chuckles*) Heh-heh-heh, heh-heh-heh, heh-heh-heh, heh-heh-heh!

COSTELLO. Fair enough. (*And launches himself into it, but it is no more than a staccato-type rattle which he is not pleased with.*)

STRANGER. Heh-heh-heh, heh-heh –

COSTELLO. No, gimme a chance, that was only a preparation.

JOHN (*to someone*). K-Costello's bet. (*beaten*)

Another attempt from COSTELLO: *it is appalling.*

STRANGER. Heh-heh-heh-heh, heh-heh-heh-heh.

COSTELLO'*s supporters are hushed and concerned for him.*

JOHN. He's b-bet.

COSTELLO *tries again: abortive.*

STRANGER. Heh-heh-heh-heh, heh-heh-heh-heh!

JOHN. B-bet. K-clown, f-fool, sis-scrounger!

MARTIN JOHN (*whispering*). Come on, Costello!

ANTHONY (*whispering*). Come on, Séamus!

BINA (*whispering*). Shout it out, Séamusheen!

JOSIE (*whispering*). Heh-hinnia!

JOHN. He's bet, b-bet, 'tis all over!

> COSTELLO *cues-in the musicians and they start to play. He tries again: fluent laughter is returning but he truncates it or lets it die. An idea is occurring to him. The* STRANGER *replies, his laugh is free, easy.*

JOHN. 'Tis all over, he has yeh done, k-codger yeh-yeh!

> COSTELLO *replies, fluently again at the start and his supporters are cheering: 'Man, Costello!' 'Up Bochtán-yahoo!' 'Hih-hinn, Costello!' But they become silent again when the laugh turns into a bout of coughing.*

COSTELLO (*coughing*). He has me bet, has he? Who says he has me bet?

JOHN. Isn't it p-plain an' k-clear he has?

COSTELLO. Is it? Will you bet on it?

JOHN (*laughs*). What have *you* to bet?

COSTELLO. The back field of mine you're always talking about. What'll you bet against it?

JOHN. Hah?

COSTELLO. What'll you bet on him beatin' me – against the field?

JOHN. Teh-teh-twenty pound.

COSTELLO. Tck! Twenty pounds an' you'll give me the shop an' throw in Rose as well.

JOHN. I'll g-give yeh g-good kick in the arse!

COSTELLO. But isn't it plain an' clear, yeh said, I'm bet already.

JOHN. An' y'are! The aul'dog (STRANGER) for the hard road.

COSTELLO. Twenty for the field if I lose, sixty-five if I win.

JOHN. Twenty for it if yeh lose, f-f-forty if you win. (*And that's his final word.*)

COSTELLO (*it's frustrating and unsatisfactory but he agrees*). Anyone else for a bet on the contest?

JOHN (*to his wife*). Write it down.

BINA. I'll bet Tufty.

COSTELLO. The cow? Again' me, Bina! An we related on me mother's side?

BINA. What can I do, Séamus? And I'd follow John Mah'ny's head any time.

COSTELLO. What's she worth t'yeh, Tufty?

BINA. Fifteen pounds, and win or lose, you'll have it from the money John'll give yeh.

COSTELLO. Done!

JOSIE. Hennia- I'll bet the clock!

COSTELLO. Stop, Josie, the clock isn't yours to bet.

JOSIE. Hinn-handiwork on it is! I'm backin' you – Heh-hinnia!

COSTELLO. What were you goin' to charge Bina for the handiwork?

JOSIE. Two-hin-thruppence.

COSTELLO. Alright. If I win you give me one and a penny-ha'penny for my trouble *and* the clock, which I'll sell to Bina for thirty bob, which she'll have from the money I give her for Tufty from what I'll get from John, win or lose, and Bina'll give you the other one an' a penny-ha'penny for your handiwork.

JOSIE. Hinnia-done!

COSTELLO. Tomás? (TOMÁS *shakes his head*.) Whatever he's (*John is*) offering for your fields, take a bit less an' back me an' you'll have your farm and the money.

JOHN. No! All d-done now.

COSTELLO (*to* TOMÁS). Wha'?

TOMÁS (No.) I'm an unlucky man, Séamus, I can't afford to gamble.

JOHN. An'-an'-an' you're a wise man.

TOMÁS. But I won't be shoutin' again yeh, Séamus!

COSTELLO (*winks at* MARTIN JOHN). All done then, Martin John?

MARTIN JOHN. The bonavs! We'll wager them on Costello, John.

JOHN. For what I offered yeh?

ANTHONY. How much did yeh offer?

MARTIN JOHN. Eight pounds.

ANTHONY. For how many of them?

JOHN. J-Jasus for the lot of them!

MARTIN JOHN. Sixteen if he wins, ten if he loses.

JOHN. You'll take ten if he wins and five if he loses. (*And he gestures 'That's it'*.)

   MARTIN JOHN *looks at* COSTELLO *and* COSTELLO *nods*.

MARTIN JOHN. Done. (*He signs the book.*)

COSTELLO. Write it all down, Rose.

JOSIE. Hinn – I'll bet me spade!

COSTELLO. Stop Josie –

JOSIE. Again' yeh, hinnia, this time!

COSTELLO. Stop, you're confusing a matter that's now clear as spring water. (*To* STRANGER.) An' nothin' at all in it for you, me little friend.

STRANGER. Heh-heh-heh-heh-heh-heh-heh!

An unsatisfactory reply from COSTELLO.

JOHN. B-bet, yeh-yeh-you're bet already. (JOHN *laughs.*) Stranger!

STRANGER. Heh-heh-heh-heh-heh-heh-heh!

COSTELLO *tries another laugh and is shaking his head and sighing in frustration. But he is shamming. He has thought of something further. He takes off one of his two top-coats, wearily, coughing. The book is brought by* JOHN'S WIFE *to* COSTELLO *for his signature.*

COSTELLO (*hesitates over signing the book*). I don't know.

JOHN. D-don't be trying to get out of it now, yeh-yeh clown-f-fool!

COSTELLO. Alright. Yeh stole one thing on me already, John Mah'ny, but you'll never steal another.

JOHN. What did I sis-steal on yeh?

COSTELLO. Which way was the way to your bed, Rose?

JOHN'S WIFE (*eyes cast down*). It was through the church, Jimmy.

COSTELLO. Was it? With the freshest featured man in Bochtán. (*To* JOHN.) Forget the back field. I'm sick of farming. And I'm sick of being called a f-fool by you. The whole farm to you for nothing if I lose.

Silence in the pub.

Are you interested?

JOHN. If-if yeh don't lose?

COSTELLO. Oh, I won't lose.

STRANGER. Heh-heh-heh-heh-heh!

JOHN. F-f-f-if yeh don't lose?

COSTELLO. I keep the farm and you'll be givin' me a hundred pounds.

JOHN. . . . He'll bate (*beat*) yeh.

COSTELLO. Oh, your little horse (STRANGER) looks confident enough.

JOHN (*yeh*) N-never wuh-won, d-did anything in your life! (COSTELLO *nods*.) F-fool yeh!

COSTELLO (*nods again*). What's a hundred pounds to a generous man like you? Sure all you're stakin' is your happiness and a lifetime of regret.

JOHN. K-k-codger!

COSTELLO. Man or mouse?

JOHN. J-Jasus Christ! – Stop! – Me head! (*His hands to his head.*)

COSTELLO. But then, you're thinkin', how much land does a man of your age need.

JOHN (*angrily*). Maybe no more than a man of your age: six by two by six!

COSTELLO. Correct.

JOHN. Hundred pounds, so b-be it, the farm to me for n-nothing if you lose. (*He has written the bet into the book.*) Write your name there. And the book will stand.

COSTELLO (*signs the book*). Oh, the book will stand.

JOHN. S-stand back now everyone. (*And give the contestants space. Gives a glass of port to his wife to take to the STRANGER'S WIFE.*) Take that over to herself, she's upsetting Costello. (*Takes a small whisky to the*

STRANGER.) An'-an' yeh won't leave this house empty-handed wh-when ye win.

COSTELLO. Are we ready?

JOHN. S-stand back everyone!

COSTELLO. Now if we only had the topic to launch us and keep us going.

STRANGER'S WIFE. Misfortunes.

STRANGER. Whist!

COSTELLO (*toasts* STRANGER). Well, here's to you, mister — bad an' all as you are!

STRANGER. And to yourself — bad an' all as I am, I'm as good as you are!

COSTELLO. We'll laugh at the music. (*He cues-in musicians. His laugh is a bit forced or tentative.*) Wo-ho-ho-ho-ho!

STRANGER. Heh-heh-heh-heh-heh-heh! (*Easy, fluent.*)

COSTELLO. Wo-ho-ho-ho-ho! (*Tentative.*)

STRANGER. Heh-heh-heh-heh-heh-heh-heh!

COSTELLO (*stops the music while he drains his glass. To himself*). Why didn't I think of this in the years gone by?

He cues-in the music and laughs. It is a great, rich, rumbling, resonant laugh, he lets it fly up to falsetto and brings it back again. There is wild cheering. The STRANGER *is laughing in admiration of* COSTELLO. *The music is lively. The* CHILD *is wide-eyed.*

ACT TWO

Before the lights come up, we hear an isolated voice in the far distance, laughing. Then another voice, calling: 'What's happening?' 'A laughing competition!' The other voice laughs: 'A what?' Other voices repeating the above, relaying the news to the surrounding countryside of what is going on in JOHN MAHONY's, the voices growing louder until we are outside the pub. We hear the STRANGER's 'Heh-heh-heh' and a chorus of laughter and cheers from outside and inside the pub at COSTELLO's reply

It is two hours later. Ideally, the pub is packed and there are more people outside. (If there is room in the pub, then, perhaps, those outside are ashamed to come in, shy, they have no money.) Those who have arrived in the last two hours are shaped and formed by poverty and hardship. Rags of clothing, deformities. But they are individual in themselves. If there is a beautiful young woman present she, too, looks freakish because of her very beauty. The sounds of sheep, goats, sea-birds can be heard in their speech and laughter. COSTELLO is king and he knows it. He caters for his minions, those outside as well as inside the pub. He takes his laugh to the door occasionally and shouts it out at those outside. He has removed his second top-coat. He is sweating.

The STRANGER, too, is sweating but he is, and he will continue to be, most in control.

JOSIE is nearly in hysterics. MARTIN JOHN and ANTHONY are wide-eyed with delight; they are also counselling TOMÁS RUA to change his mind about putting a bet on the outcome of the contest. TOMÁS RUA is beginning to wonder if he should

speculate. BINA *is urging the* STRANGER *to greater efforts.*
JOHN *is watchful. He and his wife are serving drinks.* BRIAN
coughs, 'Kuh-huchta!' and STEPHEN, *philosophically/*
funereally, to the fire, 'Oh yis!'

COSTELLO. There was a man here one time — Michael
   Corcoran — and we'd be out at night as youngsters, throwing
   stones and boodhauns at his door —

   Others have started to laugh, recognising the story.
   COSTELLO *silences them.*

   An' he'd be out after us, dancing with rage: 'I know ye well
   whoever ye are!'

   Others laughing. The line being relayed to those outside.

   Wo-ho-ho, wo-ho-ho . . . ! . . . That laugh (*Outside.*) is
   gone all the way to Dunmore!

STRANGER. Heh-heh-heh-heh-heh-heh-heh!

COSTELLO. Give us a story yourself, Mister.

STRANGER (*shaking his head, laughing.*) Heh-heh-heh-heh-
   heh-heh-heh!

BINA. Aa, God blast yeh, stranger, blast it louder back at him.

BRIAN. The one about Peader Bane, Séamus!

COSTELLO. Aw, Jesus, Peadar Bane! — Wo-ho-ho! We all
   watching him out there one day, driving the one auld sheep —
   for that was all he had. And the sheep running this way and
   that way on Peader and, says Peader — Hickle-ickle-ickle-ickle
   — says Peader — Hickle-ickle-ickle-ickle! What did Peader say?

SEVERAL VOICES. 'It's very hard to bring one of them
   together!'

   *A great response from inside and outside. The line is
   celebrated in repetition. And:*

OTHERS. Man, Costello!
On, Costello! On-on-on!
Up Bochtán!
Bochtán forever!

JOSIE. Hih-hinnia . . . !

And COSTELLO *is walking about majestically.* MARTIN
JOHN *and* ANTHONY *bring* TOMÁS RUA *to confer/
conspire with* COSTELLO, *briefly,* COSTELLO *is telling
them that in a little while he will pretend to be losing – he
bends over sideways, like a man with a pain.*

JOHN. Aa, come on, come on, k-come on, is it a contest or
isn't it? Letting other people do it for ye!

COSTELLO. Wo ho ho . . .

STRANGER. Heh heh heh . . .

COSTELLO. Throw us out another pint, John!

JOHN. It's w-waitin' for yeh, an' it's on the house. (*Gives*
COSTELLO *a pint.*)

The STRANGER *is calling for a drink but* JOHN *turns his
back on him.* JOHN *gives a glass of port to his* WIFE *and
tells her to take it to the* STRANGER'S WIFE.

COSTELLO. Well, here's to the generosity of John Mahony
again!

MARTIN JOHN. Aisy on the tack, Séamus. (*Go easy on the
drink.*)

COSTELLO (*dismissive*). Ara what! (*Drinks.*) The gallant John
Mahony over there, out courting his bride-to-be: 'There's
shtars (*stars*) up that side, he said, an' there's shtars up that
side!' – (*Upward movement of the cuffs of his jacket, wiping
his nose.*) Wo-ho-ho . . . !

STRANGER. Heh-heh-heh . . . ! A whiskey, if you please.

JOHN. D'yeh know what you're doin'? K-cause look at that child of mine there.

BINA. Or is it keepin' the throat soft y'are, Mister?

JOHN. You're pacin' yourself nicely, isn't that what you're doing?

The STRANGER *gets his whiskey and raises his glass to* COSTELLO.

COSTELLO. An' to you an' yours again! – Wo-ho-ho!

STRANGER. Heh-heh-heh, an' if mine ever come across you and yours –

COSTELLO. I hope they'll do as much for them –

STRANGER }
COSTELLO } As you and yours did for me an' mine!

They laugh together. Others laughing.

JOHN. Now, Tomás! (*He gives whiskey to* TOMÁS.)

TOMÁS RUA *slips the whiskey to* ANTHONY *who slips it into the* STRANGER's *hand a few moments later.*

Meanwhile, COSTELLO *is walking around the* STRANGER *in silence. Then, to the* STRANGER's *back, he goes:*

COSTELLO. Boo!

STRANGER. Heh-heh-heh-heh-heh-heh-heh!

COSTELLO. Well, you're the devil!

STRANGER (*walks around* COSTELLO *and, to his back, he goes*). Heh-heh-heh-heh-heh-heh-heh!

JOHN. L-laugh for laugh, K-Costello, p-play the game!

COSTELLO. Wo-ho-ho-ho-ho-ho-ho-ho! The devil.

STRANGER. I'm among friends then. Heh-heh-heh . . . !

TOMÁS RUA. I want to wager with yeh, John, after all!

JOHN. J-Jasus Christ, ye-ye're all after John's blood! An' the tricks of ye! (*Has come outside the counter to take the drink out of the* STRANGER's *hand.*)

TOMÁS. Half the price you offered me if Costello loses!

JOHN. Heedin' scallywags (MARTIN, JOHN *and* ANTHONY.) An' tryin' to get this man here drunk. (*He returns the drink to* TOMÁS RUA.) An'-an'-an' that little daughter of yours coughing knocks at death's door! K-come back to your place here, K-Costello! (*To* STRANGER.) Isn't drink tomorrow to you as good as drink today! L-laugh for l-laugh now.

COSTELLO (*returns from the doorway*). The very devil, for answer me this one, Mister –

JOSIE. Hih-hinnia-devil!

COSTELLO. Stand back, Josie! Take away the 'd' an' what have you?

STRANGER. Evil –

JOSIE. Hinnia, take away –

COSTELLO. Back, Josie! an' swing around the 'e' an' what have yeh?

STRANGER. Vile –

COSTELLO. Vile sure, yes, vile – an' take away the 'v' an' the 'e' –

STRANGER. Ill.

BINA. An' what's left without the 'I'?

STRANGER. 'L'.

COSTELLO. An' that sounds very much to me like –

ALL. Hell! (*Laughing.*) Hell! Hell!

COSTELLO. Hell an' damnation! – Wo-ho-ho-ho-ho-ho . . . !

STRANGER. Heh-heh-heh-heh-heh-heh-heh . . . !

COSTELLO (*clowning, turning circles*). Let us pause in life's pleasures, he says! (*Silence. Then:*)

COSTELLO. Wo-ho-ho-ho-ho-ho-ho!

STRANGER. Heh-heh-heh-heh-heh-heh-heh!

COSTELLO. This is gettin' serious. (*Silence. Then:*) Heh-heh-heh-heh-heh-heh-heh!

STRANGER. Heh-heh-heh-heh-heh-heh-heh!

COSTELLO (*circling, then puts his fist through the ceiling and, as if he had hurt his hand*). Ow! Boo-hoo-hoo-hoo-hoo-hoo-hoo!

STRANGER. Heh-heh-heh-heh, heh-heh-heh-heh! (*And he beats a little dance on the floor.*)

COSTELLO (*replies with a dance, his fist through the ceiling again, dances a few steps with JOHN'S WIFE: a sudden stitch in his side: he could be shamming: it's momentary*). Hickle-ickle-ickle-ickle-ickle . . . (*Falsetto.*)

The others, in chorus, laugh at the antics and exchanges and, in turn, are silent.

COSTELLO *and the* STRANGER *are laughing together. A nod from* COSTELLO *and they stop at the same moment. Their audience is puzzled.*

Hah?

Everyone laughs.

COSTELLO. Oh, true, this is serious an' I mean this is serious. (*Sternly.*) Where (are) yeh bound for, me little man, your destination, a vicko?

STRANGER. Ballindine-side, your worship. Heh-heh-heh, heh-heh-heh!

COSTELLO. Heh-heh-heh, heh-heh-heh, Ballindine-side-Mayo, a Thighearna! Cunn ether iss syha soory! (*Coinn iotair is saidhthe suaraighe.*)

BINA. Hounds of rage an' bitches of wickedness he's sayin' at you, Mister!

STRANGER. I know what he's sayin'. Heh-heh-heh-heh, heh-heh-heh-heh!

COSTELLO. Ho-ho-ho-ho-ho-ho-ho!

JOSIE. Hinn-Mayo, God help us!

JOHN. Josie, I'll – I'll put yeh out!

COSTELLO. Wo-ho-ho – Here's the health of all Ireland save County Mayo, an' them that don't like it knows where they can go! – Hickle-ickle-ickle . . . !

A reply from the STRANGER, *drowned in the laughter and cheers of the others.*

BINA. Rise it, blasht yeh, lash it back at him!

JOHN. Lave (*leave*) him alone, p-pacin' himself – Isn't that what he's – ? (*doing*)

COSTELLO. Are yeh not insulted?

STRANGER. Heh-heh-heh-heh-heh-heh-heh!

ANTHONY. Heh-heh-heh – What kind of laugh is that?

JOHN. An' was siz-size of laugh a sis-stipulation, K-Kemple?

COSTELLO *lets out a rumble of laughter,* STRANGER *replies as before.*

TOMÁS RUA. Half what you offered me, John, if Costello loses!

JOHN *grimaces, brushes the offer of the bet away from him, but, at the same time, he's not ruling it out.*

JOHN. J-Jasus, he's great – J-Jasus, your great Mister – He-he knows what he's d-doin', n-not like some of the friggin' p-plebs an' amadáns I know – 'Tis your turn, Costello, or d'yeh want more drink on the house?

COSTELLO *puts his glass on the counter for a refill. The whiskey that was taken away from the* STRANGER *earlier is slipped back to him.* COSTELLO *spits in his hands, spits on the floor.*

COSTELLO (*sternly again*). Who are yeh, a farmer?

JOSIE. Hinnia – the Devil!

JOHN. Josie! – He's f-f-friggin' farmer!

COSTELLO. A farmer?

STRANGER. A goose one.

COSTELLO. Wo-ho-ho, hickle-ickle-ickle-ickle!

JOHN (*laughing*). An' he's well able for yeh K-Costello!

COSTELLO. An' yeh sold all your cargo?

Others laughing, STRANGER *laughing.*

STRANGER. An' yourself? What're you in?

COSTELLO (*mock seriousness*). Oh now you're questioning me.

MARTIN JOHN. Rabbits, sure!

ANTHONY. Rabbits!

JOSIE. Hinnia-hull-hull-hull – !

JOHN. Josie! –

STRANGER. Rabbits! Well, heh-heh-heh, heh-heh-heh, heh-heh-heh!

COSTELLO. What's the cause of your laughter?

STRANGER. Bunny rabbits: is *that* what you're in?!

JOHN. N-now who's winnin'?

COSTELLO (*to* STRANGER). Not at all, me little man –

MARTIN JOHN. Aw, fair is fair, John! –

COSTELLO. I've a herd of Trinamanooses in Closh back the road.

STRANGER (*mock innocent face also*). Tame ones, are they?

COSTELLO. Tame ones, of a certainty, an' the finest breed for 'atin', sure.

STRANGER. But for the townies though, for city folks for 'atin'?

Their straight faces: whose face will break first?

COSTELLO. Wo-ho-ho . . . ! Give that man a drink!

STRANGER. Heh-heh-heh-heh-heh-heh-heh!

COSTELLO. Give that man a big drink!

JOSIE. Hinn – big drink! –

JOHN. No! No! –

ANTHONY. Me an' Martin John are buyin' it! –

COSTELLO. Wo-ho-ho . . . !

STRANGER. Heh-heh-heh . . . !

The movement is to the bar. JOHN *and his* WIFE *serving drinks.*

JOHN. Here, K-Costello, in spite of all your insults an' dirty talk. But that's the kind of man I am. Here, mister, an' that's your last till the contest's over. The man your k-contestin' against would drink th-the Corrib an' he'd be only wettin' his lips with it. Th-the m-mouth an' the belly on him!

BRIAN *has been out to the yard and is returning, shaking rain off himself, going to the counter.*

JOHN'S WIFE. Is it rainin' outside, Brian?

BRIAN. Kuh-hucktha, tis.

COSTELLO. Mind your fingers don't get caught in the cobwebs of your purse, Brian!

MARTIN JOHN (*aside*). Aisy on the tack, Séamus.

COSTELLO (*dismissive*). Haven't I it won? (*Catches* JOHN'S WIFE *who is taking a drink to* STRANGER'S WIFE *and dances with her.*) Rose, me thorny flower! (*Releases her and dances on his own in front of her:his virility.*) Where's me little gadhahaun of a Mayo man gone?

STRANGER. Heh-heh-heh-heh-heh-heh-heh! –

COSTELLO (*dances with* STRANGER). Heh-heh-heh-heh-heh-heh-heh, heh-heh-heh-heh-heh-heh-heh! – The poetry of John Mahony out courting his wife – (*Wiping his nose.*) 'There's shtars up that side an' there's shtars up that side'! – An' there was another man around here one time had this great taste for stealin' an' 'atin' other people's chickens –

The locals and the STRANGER *have been laughing at his performance. Renewed laughter as they recognise the story.*

Hickle-ickle-ickle-ickle!

STRANGER. Heh-heh-heh-heh-heh-heh-heh!

COSTELLO. An' he went to confession – Hickle-ickle-ickle –

STRANGER. Heh-heh-heh –

COSTELLO. An', 'Oh!' says he to the priest – 'Oh!' says he – Hickle-ickle-ickle! – 'Put as many prayers as you like on me for a penance, but don't ask me to fast.' –

STRANGER. Heh-heh-heh-heh –

COSTELLO. Hickle-ickle-ickle – 'I'm a topper at the prayin' – Wo-ho-ho – Aw, Jesus, lads, I'm kilt!' (*killed*) – 'I'm a topper at the prayin' –' Hickle-ickle-ickle – 'I'm a topper –' (*He's out of control.*)

BINA. 'I'm a topper at the prayin' but I'm a hoor at the fasting!'

All laughing.

ANTHONY. Man, Costello! –

JOSIE. Man, hinnia! –

MARTIN JOHN. Yeh have him, Séamus!

COSTELLO. Aw, Jesus, lads, I'm – Wo-ho-ho . . . !

MARTIN JOHN. Now who has it won?

JOHN. Who-who-who has it won – Is it over yet? Mister!

STRANGER. Heh-heh-heh-heh, heh-heh-heh-heh!

JOHN. There ye a-are now!

ANTHONY. Come on, Costello!

JOSIE. Hih-hinnia!

BINA. Step it up, stranger, here's luck to yeh!

JOHN. K-Costello's turn!

COSTELLO. Gimme me glass – Hickle-ickle-ickle – hand me me pint – Wo-ho-ho . . . !

STRANGER. Heh-heh-heh-heh-heh-heh-heh!

COSTELLO has his hand raised for silence.

COSTELLO. Point of information. An' just to show I'm not stoppin' for ulterior motivations, as the fella says, here's one: Wo-ho-ho-ho-ho-ho-ho-hickle-ickle-ickle-ickle . . . ! Now, the question is, *how*, how is it to be indisputably decided who is the winner?

JOHN. Oh, sh-sh-sh-sure – Hah?

COSTELLO. Indisputably the winner. (*And he nods solemnly.*)

Silence.

STEPHEN (*to the fire*). 'Tis a difficult question.

STRANGER'S WIFE. . . . . He who laughs last.

STRANGER. Ar . . .

About to reprimand her — 'Stop' or 'Whist' — but she is smiling at him very softly and, without knowing why, he smiles back at her.

COSTELLO. That's — that's what I thought.

COSTELLO spits on the floor. He paws at the spit with his boot. There is something of a lost bull about him.

JOHN (*quietly*). Mister.

STRANGER. Heh-heh-heh-heh-heh-heh-heh!

STRANGER'S WIFE *laughs.*

JOHN. . . . (*Quietly.*) Costello's turn.

COSTELLO. Wait'll I think of another . . . (*story*)

ANTHONY (*whispering*). He's lost it.

STEPHEN. Oh yis.

MARTIN JOHN (*whispering*). Come on, Séamus.

ANTHONY (*whispering*). He never should have stopped.

JOSIE. Hih-hinnnnn.

BRIAN. Kuh-hucktha.

MARTIN JOHN. Rise up the music —

Musicians play quietly —

Try a few more riddles, Séamus! —

ANTHONY. Give him a bar of a song, Bina!

JOHN. She won't!

BINA. I won't!

JOHN. N-n-no favouritism! — He's bet! —

MARTIN JOHN. Come on, stranger, throw in a laugh to help him out!

STRANGER. Heh-heh-heh –

JOHN. No! L-laugh for l-l-l- Now, d'ye know!

COSTELLO. Permission to go out the back!

JOHN. No!

COSTELLO. Oh? Did yeh sis-stipulate that we have to do it on the floor?

People chuckling.

COSTELLO *looks at the* STRANGER *for the* STRANGER's *permission.*

STRANGER. To be sure.

COSTELLO. Thank you. (*To* JOHN.) Now d'yeh know! (*Going out.*) Make way! I'm goin' out to shoot a few crows in the yard. (*Fart. And he laughs going out the back door.*)

JOHN. An' my little horse wuh-will be waitin' for yeh when yeh get back – wh-when yeh get back!

And he laughs harshly after COSTELLO. *He has taken a few steps after* COSTELLO. *He nods to himself, he believes that* COSTELLO *has had it.*

MARTIN JOHN (*to himself*). Aw Jasus, well if Costello isn't the right hoor! (*To* TOMÁS RUA *and* ANTHONY.) It's the signal. He's pullin', like he said he would. Now's your chance, Tomás, to try the Sheik (JOHN) again . . . . . .

They are conferring and, through the following, they approach JOHN *and we see the bet being struck and being entered in the book.*

The STRANGER'S WIFE *is smiling: he goes to her:*

STRANGER. Ar, whist. Heh-heh-heh-heh! What's come over us?

She starts to laugh with him, quietly. They stop. Tears brim to her eyes. The misfortunes of a lifetime.

Ar, Bridget . . .

She titters again. He laughs with her.

STRANGER'S WIFE. I see the animals in the field look more fondly on each other than we do.

STRANGER. It's rainin'. The thaw is set in. Shouldn't we be goin'?

STRANGER'S WIFE (*shakes her head, no*). . . . How long since we laughed or looked upon each other before?

STRANGER (*nods. Laughs quietly. His laugh, like hers, near tears*). . . . But shouldn't we go?

STRANGER'S WIFE. No . . . An' you have him bet.

She embraces him. They start to sway, as in a dance. It is like as if they have forgotten everyone around them in this moment.

STRANGER. But 'twas only the comicalest notion that comes into a person's head. Heh-heh-heh.

STRANGER'S WIFE. Whatever it was, you have them bet. We've been defeated in all else but this one thing we'll win.

They separate. The STRANGER chuckles, perhaps a little embarrassed.

You'll get him with misfortunes.

COSTELLO has returned, he doesn't look well but he's trying to cover it.

JOHN. Now! The heh-hero is back! (*Derisively.*)

COSTELLO *striding to his pint to drink. Murmers of
encouragement from his supporters.*

MARTIN JOHN (*aside to* COSTELLO). Well, if you aren't the
greatest hoor in creation.

TOMÁS RUA (*smiling, his sickly daughter,* PEGGY, *beside
him*). I've me place on yeh, Séamus.

COSTELLO *is frightened, drains his glass:*

COSTELLO. Right! Are yeh ready? What's the topic?

STRANGER. Misfortunes. Heh-heh-heh-heh-heh!

COSTELLO. *What* misfortunes?!

JOSIE *goes 'Hih-hinnia',* PEGGY *starts coughing,* TOMÁS
RUA *puts his one good arm around her and chuckles,
someone else limps in or out, the* STRANGER'S WIFE *is
laughing. The forgotten and neglected peasantry, chuckling.*
COSTELLO *doesn't understand, but he starts to chuckle,
'What?', in incomprehension, like a man in a nightmare. The
laughter of the others grows in volume to complement him.
He becomes silent, the laughter of the others dying.*

The STRANGER *laughs.*

COSTELLO *taking off his jacket. His arms tangled in the
sleeve, he can't get it off.* JOHN *is laughing derisively at him,
the others are laughing.* PEGGY *is laughing.* COSTELLO,
*arms, jacket, a pullover caught in the jacket, moves almost on
top of* PEGGY *and* TOMÁS RUA, *his load above their heads,
as if he wanted to bring his load down on top of them to
smother them.*

JOHN. K-clown, p-pleb, f-fool, he's bet!

COSTELLO *sends his jacket and pullover into a corner and is
making for* JOHN. *He looks dangerous.*

JOSIE. Hinn – take – off – hinn – (your) trousers, Costello!

Suddenly COSTELLO *has* JOSIE *by the throat. And now, for a moment, he can't think of a reason for his action.* JOSIE *can hardly breathe.*

Hnnnnn . . . !

COSTELLO. Gimme the clock, I said!

JOSIE. Hnnnnn –

COSTELLO. I'm not askin'!

JOSIE *gives him the clock (the usual cheap clock found on mantelpieces in country kitchens).* COSTELLO *listens to it, shakes, etc.*

It's well mended alright. That clock now, I would say, will go for a year without stoppin', standing on the mantelpiece, an' maybe for two more lyin' on its face. (*He doesn't know what he's talking about.*)

JOSIE. Hih-hnn – finest clock – (*Perhaps 'in the world'.*)

COSTELLO. But the question is . . . the question is, can it fly?

A gasp from the others because his arm is aloft to throw the clock. Then the alarm goes off, startling him – 'Oh Jesus!' – making him drop the clock, making him laugh.

JOSIE, *who is on his knees, catches the clock and, a moment later,* BINA *takes it from him.*

COSTELLO'*s big laugh from the fright he has had, the others laughing with him, as is* JOSIE, *innocently, and as is the* STRANGER.

Right! – (*To* STRANGER.) Are yeh sure yeh don't want to withdraw?

STRANGER'S WIFE. There's no one withdrawin' unless it's yourself, big man from Bochtán!

COSTELLO. An' yeh sold all your cargo?

STRANGER'S WIFE. Yeh said that!

COSTELLO. An' did yeh sell the geese last year?

STRANGER. No.

COSTELLO. Oh?

STRANGER. The fox got the lot of them — Heh-heh-heh-heh . . . !

COSTELLO. Wo-ho-ho-ho — I understand yeh now, ma'am — misfortunes — the fox got — Wo-ho-ho . . . . ! An' the potatoes!

STRANGER. The potatoes?

ANTHONY. How were they for yeh?

BRIAN. The damnable crop was in it this year.

STRANGER. The potatoes, oh, heh-heh, heh-heh-heh, heh-heh-heh!

COSTELLO. Wet an' watery — Wo-ho-ho —

STRANGER. Soapy an' sour — Heh-heh-heh —

COSTELLO. But not blighted, d'yeh tell me? —

STRANGER. (No, but) Scabby an' small —

COSTELLO. Thin on the ground — Wo-ho-ho —

STRANGER. Hard to dig — Heh-heh-heh —

COSTELLO. Hard to wash, ladies, hard to boil, ladies? —

BINA. An' the divil to ate!

All laughing. Laughing through the following and the contestants swapping laughs.

BRIAN. An' the hay, behell!

COSTELLO | Rotted!
STRANGER |

MARTIN JOHN. The bita oats — Jasus!

TOMÁS RUA. Lodged in the field!

ANTHONY. The barley! —

OTHERS. The same!

BRIAN. Well-mildewed, the straw!

COSTELLO. An' the turf for the fire, Stephen?!

OTHERS. Still in the bog!

BINA. An' th'aul cow, mister?!

STRANGER. Aw, th'aul cow is still in it!

MARTIN JOHN. An' the sheep! –

COSTELLO. The staggers!

BINA. An' the chickens, the pip!

TOMÁS RUA. An' did we ever before see a summer like it?

STEPHEN (*rising*). Oh we did.

BRIAN. Kuh-hucktha, hah?

STEPHEN (*funereally, going out*). Last winter. (*He returns sometime later, shaking the rain off him.*)

COSTELLO. An' your arm, Tomás Rua?!

TOMÁS RUA. Lost to the thresher!

JOSIE. Eye-hinnia-eye! (*Pointing to* BINA.)

COSTELLO. An' your eye, Bina?!

BINA. A hoor of a briar!

STRANGER'S WIFE. An' the dead!

The momentum carries the laughter forward.

COSTELLO. An' the dead – Wo-ho-ho! – An' the dead, ma'am? Me father, is it, you're referring to? Sure, he killed himself, sure: drowned himself in the barrel at the gable-end of the house. 'Twas a difficult feat?

STRANGER. Heh-heh-heh-heh-heh-heh-heh!

COSTELLO. Wo-ho-ho-ho-ho . . . ! An' yourself, ma'am?

STRANGER'S WIFE. Hih-hih-hih – I had nine sons –

STRANGER. Heh-heh-heh-heh-heh-heh-heh!

STRANGER'S WIFE. An' for the sake of an aul' ewe was stuck in the flood was how I lost Jimmy an' Michael – Hih-hih-hih!

COSTELLO. Wo-ho-ho . . . ! – For the sake of an aul' ewe!

STRANGER. Heh-heh-heh . . . !

STRANGER'S WIFE. An' the nice wife Jimmy left behind, died, tryin' to give birth to the fourth child that was to be in it – Bate (*beat*) that! Hih-hih-hih!

COSTELLO. Oh, sure – Wo-ho-ho . . . ! – Many's the one from here was lost to the water –

STRANGER'S WIFE. An' Pat who was my first born –

STRANGER } Heh-heh-heh . . . !
STRANGER'S WIFE } Married the widdy against my wishes.

COSTELLO. Wo-ho-ho . . . !

STRANGER'S WIFE. The decline (TB) in that family! –

OTHERS. The decline! The decline!

STRANGER'S WIFE. An' when he came back for the two sheep (that) were his –

STRANGER. Heh-heh-heh . . . !

STRANGER'S WIFE. You'll not have them, I told him, and sent him back, lame, to his strap of a widdy –

COSTELLO. Wo-ho-ho . . . !

STRANGER'S WIFE. An' he was dead within a six months – Hih-hih-hih! – Bate that!

COSTELLO. Oh, sure – Hickle-ickle-ickle . . . !

OTHERS. Man, Costello!
On, Costello!
Up Bochtán, on Bochtán!
Bochtán forever!

COSTELLO. Oh sure – Hickle-ickle-ickle-ickle . . . !

STRANGER. Heh-heh-heh . . . !

COSTELLO. Oh, sure, the decline – TB – lost to the water – tuberculosis – lost across the sea, in England –

STRANGER'S WIFE } An' America! –
STRANGER   } An' America!

STRANGER'S WIFE. One after the other!

COSTELLO. One after the other! –

STRANGER'S WIFE. Never to be heard of ever again – Hih-hih-hih!

COSTELLO. Wo-ho-ho, hickle-ickle-ickle . . . !

STRANGER. Heh-heh-heh . . . !

STRANGER'S WIFE. The unbaptised an' still-born –

COSTELLO. The unbaptised an' still-born –

STRANGER'S WIFE. Buried in unconsecrated ground – Hih-hih-hih! –

COSTELLO. In shoe-boxes planted – Many's the neighbour I went with – Hickle-ickle-ickle! – Didn't we Martin John?

MARTIN JOHN. At the dead hour of night – Jasus! –

COSTELLO. Treading softly the Lisheen –

MARTIN JOHN. That field haunted by infants –

COSTELLO. Too afeared to speak or pray –

STRANGER'S WIFE. Ye were fearful for yere ankles – Hih-hih-hih.

STRANGER. Heh-heh-heh . . . !

COSTELLO. Wo-ho-ho, hickle-ickle . . . !

   Others cheering COSTELLO.

   Jasus, misfortunes, wo-ho-ho . . . !

BINA. Come on, Mister, rise it! – Pneumonia, Scarletina!

MARTIN JOHN. Double pneumonia! – Séamus!

COSTELLO. Treble it! – Wo-ho-ho . . . !

JOHN. F-f-fever, Mister!

BINA. The chin-cough! –

STRANGER. Dip'teria – Heh-heh-heh . . . !

JOSIE. Hinn-chicken-bones! (*Choking on them.*) –

TOMÁS RUA. Pleurisy! –

COSTELLO. Meningitis! – Hickle-ickle . . . !

STRANGER'S WIFE. Per'tonitis! – Hih-hih-hih.

BRIAN. The 'looseness' –

STRANGER. Heh-heh-heh – Diarrhoea! – Heh-heh-heh . . . !

COSTELLO. Dysentery, malaria, a stroke! – Hickle-ickle . . . !

JOSIE. Hinnia-chicken bones!

STRANGER'S WIFE. Now, is that the topic? – Hih-hih-hih!

COSTELLO. That surely is the topic! –

STRANGER. Heh-heh-heh . . . !

COSTELLO. Wo-ho-ho, hickle-ickle . . .

TOMÁS RUA. Misfortunes!

COSTELLO. The still-born an' forlorn, he says! – Wo-ho-ho . . . !

STRANGER. The lonely an' bereaved! – Heh-heh-heh . . . !

COSTELLO. The half-starved, half-demented! – Hickle-ickle . . . !

OTHERS. Those lost to America!
  Arms lost to the thresher!
  Suicide an' bad weather!
  Blighted crops!
  Bad harvests!

Bad markets!
How to keep the one foot in front of the other!
Per'tonitis!
An' fever, yellow, black an' scarlet!
Chicken-bones!
Briars to take out your eyes!
Or to bate the children with!
Put smacht (*manners*) on them when there's nought for their
bellies!
Miadh, misfortunes!
An' there's more to come!

STRANGER'S WIFE. Send them! (*To the heavens.*)

COSTELLO. Oh, there's more to come!

OTHERS. Send them!

STRANGER. We're waitin'!

COSTELLO. We are!

OTHERS. We are!

STRANGER. For anything else to come, or might care to come!

COSTELLO (*like the others, shouting at the heavens*). Send us
your best!

*All shouting, their heads thrown back in defiant laughter –
except* JOHN, STEPHEN *and, perhaps, the* CHILD *who is
agog. Fists are puncturing the ceiling, feet stamping the floor.*

JOHN. Are ye t-t-temptin' the Almighty? Stand back, clear
back, let the k-contest continue! No-no-no-no more drink till
the contest is decided. An'-an' temptin' God's goodness! Have
ye forgot what's at stake? . . . D'ye know now.

A kind of order is gradually achieved. Now we see
COSTELLO, *doubled-up, straightening-up, loosening his
buckle, opening down his shirts, holding his sides, staggering*

about. He is now, all the time, in the upper register – 'Hickle-ickle' – He cannot stop it.

The STRANGER, *too, is holding his sides and doubling-up occasionally. But there is a stillness coming over him, a concern and a fear as he watches* COSTELLO *changing colour.*

COSTELLO. Hickle-ickle-ickle-ickle . . . !

STRANGER. Heh-heh-heh-heh-heh-heh!

COSTELLO. Hickle-ickle-ickle-ickle . . . !

OTHERS. Man, Costello! Man, Séamus!

BINA. More power to yeh, stranger!

JOHN. Now, Mister, again!

STRANGER. Heh-heh-heh-heh-heh-heh-heh!

COSTELLO. Aw Jasus, lads – (*A fit of coughing.*)

JOHN. N-now, Mister, in quick again!

STRANGER. Heh-heh-heh-heh-heh-heh-heh!

COSTELLO. Hickle-ickle-ickle-ickle – Aw Jays, lads, I'm – Hickle-ickle-ickle-ickle!

JOHN. Now, m-Mister, again!

STRANGER. Heh-heh-heh-heh-heh-heh-heh!

COSTELLO. Hickle-ickle-ickle-ickle – Aw Jays, lads, I'm – Hickle-ickle-ickle-ickle!

JOHN. Now, m-Mister, again!

STRANGER. Heh-heh-heh-heh-heh-heh-heh!

COSTELLO. Hickle-ickle-ickle-ickle – (*His hand up to call a stop, but he can barely raise his arms.*)

MARTIN JOHN. Lave (*leave*) the ceiling to us, Séamus!
(*Punching the ceiling, as is* ANTHONY.)

ANTHONY. Come on, Costello!

TOMÁS RUA. Come on, Costello!

JOHN. M-mister!

BINA. Stranger!

STRANGER. Heh-heh-heh-heh . . . heh-heh-heh!

COSTELLO. Aw, Jays, lads, I'm – Hickle-ickle-ickle –

*He is falling over himself, occasionally leaning on someone
for support. Every time, he is pushed back into the 'arena'.*

An' the rabbits, lads – Hickle-ickle-ickle-ickle!

JOHN. N-now, Mister, in at him again!

COSTELLO. An' the rabbits, lads – Aw Jasus – Hickle-ickle-
ickle-ickle!

BINA. Answer him, stranger!

JOHN. R-r-reply, mister!

COSTELLO. I didn't sell e'er the one of them – Aw Jasus, lads,
I'm dyin' – but threwn them comin' home for fun agin' Patch
Curran's door! Hickle-ickle-ickle . . . !

OTHERS. Yahoo! Yahoo!
On, Costello, you have him!
On Bochtán!
Up Bochtán!
Bochtán forever! (*Etc.*)

STRANGER. Heh-heh-heh! (*Quietly, the two little smiles on
the corners of his mouth.*)

BINA. Blasht yeh, stranger, louder!

STRANGER. Stop! Costello's the winner!

OTHERS	Yahoo, (etc.)
STRANGER'S WIFE	He's nat (not), he's nat, he's nat, he's nat!
JOHN	N-not, f-false, he's not!
BINA	He's not!

COSTELLO *and the* STRANGER *are now together in the centre of the floor,* COSTELLO *supporting himself on the* STRANGER's *shoulders.*

STRANGER. Stop, man, stop.

COSTELLO. Hickle-ickle-ickle – I can't – hickle-ickle . . . !

STRANGER. Heh-heh-heh-heh-heh-heh-heh!

BINA. Good on yeh, God bless yeh, stranger!

JOHN. N-n-now! Now!

STRANGER. Costello's the – (*winner*).

COSTELLO. Hickle-ickle-ickle-ickle . . . !

STRANGER. Heh-heh-heh-heh-heh – Stand up straight, your full height, I'll not laugh anymore.

COSTELLO *is embracing the* STRANGER – *they are like two people in a slow dance –* COSTELLO's *'hickle-ickle' continues but he now appears to be whispering to the* STRANGER. *The* STRANGER *appears to nod to what is being whispered; he appears to be close to tears.*

COSTELLO's *laughter peters out.*

STRANGER. Heh-heh-heh-heh-heh-heh-heh!

The two of them collapse on the floor, COSTELLO, *face down, across the* STRANGER's *legs, the* STRANGER *sitting up.*

The noise subsides to silence.

JOHN. Ih-ih-ih-is he . . . is he?

JOSIE (*quietly*). Hinnnnnn! (*Crouches down, shakes* COSTELLO's *foot.*) Hinnnnnn . . . !

JOHN. G-g-go for the priest, one of ye. L-last laugh. The book h-has to stand.

JOSIE is crying at death and becoming excited: the STRANGER is the Devil, the STRANGER'S WIFE is the Devil's wife: the boots have to be taken off the STRANGER to prove it, i.e., that the STRANGER has hooves, not feet.

JOSIE. Hinn-Devil, Hinn-Devil's wife — Hinn-boots off —

JOHN. Come on, Josie, a mac *(son)* —

JOSIE is tugging at the STRANGER's boots and swiping at the STRANGER. The STRANGER is trying to get up. The others are pressing forward: confused, becoming wild-eyed, beginning to make low, angry sounds. JOHN, with his book, pulling JOSIE back.

JOSIE. Hinn-boots? till we see if he has feet in them! —

JOHN. G-go, Mister — Sis-sis-stop, Josie —

One of JOSIE's swings sends the book flying out of JOHN's hands. JOHN falls back against the others, one of his arms catching ANTHONY in the mouth, the other catching BINA. Someone else catches someone else. JOHN, coming forward to retrieve his book, is sent sprawling over JOSIE and COSTELLO by MARTIN JOHN . . . Mayhem breaks loose. Clamouring, shouting, things are broken. STRANGER and his WIFE trying to defend themselves, getting out the door. The melée goes out the door. Only the CHILD remains, looking at the prone body of COSTELLO.

Voices outside:

VOICES. Hinnia — Devil!
Go, yeh devil yeh!
An' bad luck to ye!
Skelong!

STRANGER'S WIFE. An' 'tis glad we are to be goin' from the rogues and thieves that parade Bochtán an' the villainy of Galway!

VOICES. Pull them down off the cart!
  Jasus, d'ye hear them!
  Give him the kickin'!
  That's it, welt him!
  L-let them go, let them off!
  Ye unholy couple!
  Skelong, skelong!
  An' never come back!
  Hounds of rage, bitches of wickedness!
  Bad luck to ye!

The horse and cart moving off: as it fades.

Heh-heh-heh-heh-heh-heh-heh!

*During the last, the CHILD puts his fingers in his mouth:
COSTELLO stirs. The CHILD runs out to his parents who
are coming in with the others. COSTELLO is at death's door
but he isn't dead.*

MARTIN JOHN. Aw, Jasus, no, John, nothing stands –

TOMÁS RUA. Aw, God, no, John –

ANTHONY. Sure all must be declared null an' void.

MARTIN JOHN. A man is dead.

JOHN. An'-an'-an' the h-heavens be his bed – But huh-who
  laughed last? – The b-book stands. Now d'ye know.

*The CHILD finally draws their attention to COSTELLO who
has raised himself up a little.*

COSTELLO. Wo-ho-ho-ho-ho-ho-ho . . . !

Silence.

JOSIE. Hih-hinn?

STEPHEN. Oh yis!

BRIAN. Kuh-huckta!

MARTIN JOHN. The book stands.

ANTHONY. Yeh owe us ten pounds.

TOMÁS RUA. Yeh owe me a lot more.

BINA. An' I lost nothin'. Fifteen pounds out of what yeh owe Costello for me cow.

JOSIE. Hinnia-one-penny – ha'penny.

JOHN. J-Jasus, me head! J-Jasus, Costello, an' th'the priest comin' to send you off!

They put COSTELLO *in a chair.*

COSTELLO. I'm goin' (*dying*). You'll give the hundred pounds to me mother.

JOHN. 'T-'t'll be honoured. 't'll be honoured.

COSTELLO. Wo-ho-ho! An' that's the last laugh.

JOHN. An'-an'-an' that'll be honoured too, k-cause if I ever hear as much as a-a – (giggle) – in here ever again, I'll-I'll-I'll!

COSTELLO. I always had a wish to see a bit of me own Wake. Let ye begin till I see what it's like.

The music starts up. People are buying rounds of drink. The Wake is lively. JOSIE *is bringing a pint to* COSTELLO *but* COSTELLO's *head has fallen to one side. He's dead .* JOSIE *sits on the floor beside* COSTELLO's *chair.*